Following Jesus

Sermons on Discipleship

Following Jesus

Sermons on Discipleship from Pastors and Professors

W. Hulitt Gloer
Editor

Smyth & Helwys Publishing, Inc.
Macon, Georgia

ISBN 880837-36-6

Following Jesus:
Sermons on Discipleship from Pastors and Professors
edited by W. Hulitt Gloer

Copyright © 1994
Smyth & Helwys Publishing, Inc.

The paper used in this publication meets the minimum
requirements of American Standard for Information
Sciences—Permanence of paper for Printed Library Materials,
ANSI Z39.48–1984.

Library of Congress Cataloging-in-Publication Data

Following Jesus : sermons on discipleship from pastors and
professors / W. Hulitt Gloer, editor.
    x + 168 pp.   6 x 9" (15 x 23 cm.)
    ISBN 880837-36-6
    1. Christian life—Sermons.   2. Sermons, American.   3.
Baptists—Sermons. 4. Southern Baptist Convention—Sermons.
I. Gloer, Hulitt.
BX6333.A1F64 1993
252'.061—dc20
                                               93-34361
                                                  CIP

Contents

Editor's Preface vii

1. On Being Worth Your Salt 1
   Fred Andrea

2. What is God Doing in the Storm? 7
   Gerald Borchert

3. Reverence, Revision, and Redeeming Love 13
   Linda McKinnish Bridges

4. Discipleship: A Markan Perspective 21
   Donald E. Cook

5. A Standing Exam for Servants of God 29
   Bruce Corley

6. The Second Call, the Second Baptism 35
   R. Alan Culpepper

7. Surviving the Test 45
   Paul D. Duke

8. Getting into the Boat 51
   David E. Garland

9. Take Up the Towel. . . . Take Up the Cross! 59
   W. Hulitt Gloer

10. Will the Real Minister Please Stand Up? 65
    John H. Hewett

11. The Unshakable Kingdom 73
    D. Leslie Hollon

12. Drop Everything! 81
     David M. Hughes

13. Alternatives to Anxiety 89
     Peter Rhea Jones

14. Peter the Disciple 99
     Michael Martin

15. An Invitation to Discipleship 107
     David M. May

16. Following Jesus, Parts I & II 115
     H. Stephen Shoemaker

17. Look Again 129
     R. Wayne Stacy

18. An Affirmation of Faith 137
     Jon M. Stubblefield

19. Catching People 145
     James A. Weaver

20. Possessions 153
     Kenneth R. Wolfe

Contributors 161

Preface

In the year 1896 a Kansas pastor published a little book that was destined to become a devotional classic. The pastor's name was Charles Sheldon. The book was called *In His Steps*. Since its publication almost a century ago, *In His Steps* has sold more than 30,000,000 copies and despite the fact that its setting is vintage turn-of-the-century Americana, it has been translated into more than 20 languages. The publisher's introduction to the 1973 reprint suggests that the book "deserves a place among great religious books not because it represents impeccable literary craftsmanship but because it clings to the idea and ideal that captured the imagination of millions-[that] the teaching of Jesus Christ is indeed practical and workable if fearlessly put to the test."[1] That test, according to Sheldon, is simply this: before every undertaking ask this question, "What would Jesus do?" Sheldon's narration of the revolutionary consequences that ensue when the people of a fictional American town set out to apply this test has been called a "novelistic essay on modern Christian discipleship,"[2] and while it has often been criticized as too simplistic, the continuing popularity of the book is evidence of the fact that the fundamental issue that confronts every generation of believers is this: What does it mean to be a disciple of Jesus?

Surely there is no more important question than this for the Christian individually and for the church corporately. In their stimulating book *Resident Aliens*, Stanley Hauerwas and William Willimon remind us that "With a simple 'follow me,' Jesus invited ordinary people to come out and be part of an adventure, a journey that kept surprising them at every turn in the road."[3] What, then, is the meaning of this "simple 'follow me' "? How are we to understand this adventure? What is the nature of this journey on which Jesus would lead us individually and corporately as His church? Hauerwas and Willimon go on to remind us that ". . . the task of the church is the formation of a people who see clearly the cost of discipleship and are willing to pay the price."[4] But just what is "the cost of discipleship"? What is the price we are called to pay? Through the centuries answers to this question have ranged from the rigid asceticism and isolationism of the Desert

Fathers of the second and third centuries to the radical activism of twentieth century liberation theologians. And still the question remains: What *does* it mean to be a disciple of Jesus?

While the New Testament portrayal of Jesus has come to us in four quite distinctive presentations, all four gospels agree that the essence of Jesus' call to his first followers is summarized in the command "follow me." When Jesus confronted those who would be his first disciples, he did not produce a creed and say, "If you can accept these propositions, then you can be my disciple." He said, "Follow me!" When Jesus stopped in the doorway of Levi's tax office, he did not say, "If you have a certain kind of emotional catharsis, then you can be my disciple." He said, "Follow me!" This was the call to discipleship then. This is the call to discipleship now. It is, indeed, the call to walk "in His steps." Still the question remains, "What does it mean to follow Jesus?"

The purpose of this collection of sermons is to enable readers to hear the call to discipleship once again in clear and fresh tones. Over the past decade we have seen a renewed interest in the whole matter of discipleship. Among Southern Baptists, Church Training has become Discipleship Training and the 1990s designated the Decade of Discipleship. Christian bookstores have been inundated with "how-to" books and denominations have developed and promoted all manner of discipleship programs. Yet an examination of much of the popular material treating discipleship reveals that it is often quite shallow focusing on emphases and practices that receive little if any attention in the teaching of Jesus, while emphases and practices that seem central to Jesus' teaching are never even mentioned! These sermons aim at setting the New Testament emphases before us. They are meant to be read and pondered as part of the ongoing struggle to understand more fully what it means to be a disciple of Jesus in today's world. It is our prayer that the experience of reading these sermons will enable you to *see* the Christ more clearly, *love* Him more dearly and *follow* Him more nearly day by day. Together let us seek to be that people who see clearly the cost of discipleship and are willing to pay the price!

W. Hulitt Gloer
January 1993

Notes

[1]The quotation from the 1973 reprinted is cited by John Elliot, "Backward and Forward 'In His Steps': Following Jesus from Rome to Raymond and Beyond—The Tradition, Redaction and Reception of 1 Peter 2:18-25," in *Discipleship in the New Testament*, ed. Fernando Segovia (Philadelphia: Fortress Press, 1985) 184.

[2]Ibid.

[3]Stanley Hauerwas and William Willimon, *Resident Aliens* (Nashville: Abingdon Press, 1989) 49.

[4]Ibid., 60.

On Being Worth Your Salt

Matthew 5:13-16

Fred Andrea

For several years, I met different friends and colleagues for breakfast at Gene's Restaurant. There in the middle of various modern office buildings, with all their carpeted offices, Gene's Restaurant represents the best of days gone by—tile floor, booths with formica top tables, and an atmosphere that feels like every small town eating establishment you have entered in your whole life.

The best part of Gene's Restaurant for me has been an employee named Goldie. She went to work over there about the same time I discovered the place. She looks a good deal older than my mother, and is the only one who has taken my breakfast order there in years. "You want any coffee, honey?" she inquired of me when I arrived last Friday. "How about you, sweetie?" she asked my friend when he walked in a few minutes later.

Goldie talks to everyone that way, and through her intimacy and warmth the less than bright decorum of the restaurant itself is transcended by the color of her personality. "Want your coffee warmed up, sugar?" she asked several times. On each occasion we both said enthusiastically, "Sure!" Who can turn down an offer like that? We drank so much coffee that both of us just floated back to the office!

I know nothing about Goldie except that she is a widow and that she always brings the pie to the customer before she brings the salad. That ensures they get the dessert before the kitchen crew runs out of pie! You can understand why so many people love and appreciate her. She adds a little spice to everybody's day.

There we sat at 7:00 Friday morning. It was the end of a long, exhausting week. The sky was still a bit dark and the weather on the outside was cold and rainy. But the forecast on the inside was bright and sunny. Goldie was doing her "thing." You really ought to try a meal there sometime, especially the breakfast. The food is pretty good, and Goldie is even better. In my book, she is a person who is worth her salt.

"Worth her salt"—that expression has been around a long time. Salt has served in the past and still serves in the present as a precious commodity in life. Salt is still used as a form of currency in Tibet and parts of Africa.

In the days of Jesus, the Greeks considered salt to be divine. Working people and soldiers of ancient Greece and Rome were often paid some or even all of their wages in salt. As a result, compensation for labor became known as *salarium*, Latin for "salt money." When we say people are worth their salt, we say they have earned their money and performed their tasks well.

It comes as no shock, then, that Jesus used salt as a way of talking about discipleship. It was as common as life itself, and everybody knew of its value. "You are the salt of the earth," he said to those who wanted to follow him. That meant, of course, that Jesus accepted no people as his ambassadors unless they were really worth their salt.

Just thinking about the way in which salt adds flavor to life, it is no surprise that Christians are called to live in such a way that we add zest and vitality to everybody's existence. There is nothing drab or somber about being disciples of Jesus. Living out our Christian faith provides the most exciting and electrifying opportunities on the earth.

A man was approached at an airport terminal and asked, "Are you the minister I am supposed to pick up?" "No," the gentleman replied, "I just got a little air sick on the plane." As long as there are people who think Christians are anemic and lacking in joy, as long as people equate being boring with being blessed, we will need to remember and to live like we are the "salt of the earth." Salt adds flavor and spice to everyone's life; so does the Christian faith. "You are the salt of the earth, " Jesus said.

Then, too, salt is a preservative. It keeps things from going rotten or from giving in to decay. Plutarch, the ancient Greek essayist and biographer, once observed that meat was a dead body and that part of a dead body, if left to itself, would certainly go bad. But, he added, salt preserves meat, keeps it fresh, and works like a soul inserted into a dead body.

Given all the moral, ethical, economic, and political decay going on throughout this nation and across the world, Christians need desperately through our witness to retard that process and through the quality of our living keep the entire world from going rotten. There is plenty of death around us into which a soul needs to be implanted. Our living as the "salt of the earth" will do precisely that.

We can all think of people who have known whose sense of right or wrong was so strong that just being in their presence made you want to do your best and to do battle with the worst. An elementary teacher, a coach in middle school, your adviser in high school, the woman who taught you in Sunday School (I can still remember the day when my Sunday School teacher stared at me and said, "Fred, Jesus and I are very disappointed in you!" That will straighten up your life in a hurry.), the man who lived next door, your mom or dad, one of your grandparents—silently name that person to yourself.

They helped preserve the integrity of your life and motivated you to preserve society's values through your living. They were ordinary folk with an extraordinary faith. They were people really worth their salt. People like that make the world a better place.

That is why, after we gather here for worship every Sunday, we scatter out to serve God's Kingdom through this region. God needs salt in every part of the world in order for it to be preserved. Through our daily activities, God helps preserve the sanctity of life in and around Savannah, Georgia.

When I was at the Southern Baptist Theological Seminary, I heard a minister from England preach on this particular scripture text. He used a different image to tell those of us in seminary what it meant for Jesus to call us the "salt of the earth." "Ministers," he said, "are like manure. Spread them out across the earth and they produce a bountiful harvest. But put them all together in the same place at the same time, and yuck!"

Lay persons are just the same. We are productive only when we go out to all parts of the earth and share our faith in day-to-day living. That is how we preserve God's creation. "You are the salt of the earth," said Jesus. The question is, "Are we really worth our salt?"

Look with me again at the fifth chapter of Matthew's Gospel. Generally, the first twelve verses are taken as a unit, and verses 13 through 16 a second unit. At first glance Matthew 5:1–11 is a unified passage because each verse starts with "blessed." "Blessed are the poor in spirit, . . . blessed are those who mourn, . . . blessed are the meek, . . . blessed are those who hunger and thirst after righteousness, . . . blessed are the merciful, . . . blessed are the pure in heart, . . . blessed are the peacemakers, . . . blessed are those who are persecuted for righteousness' sake. . . ."

But look at that next verse. "Blessed are you . . ." it says. There is a change from the third person to the second person. That entire verse reads: "Blessed are you when people revile you and persecute you and utter all kinds of evil against you falsely on my account." The use of the second person brings Matthew 5:11 closer in emphasis to the verses I read to you earlier, Matthew 5:13–16. Verse 13 says, "You are the salt of the earth. . . ." Verse 14 claims, "You are the light of the world. . . ." Verse 16 challenges, "Let your light so shine. . . ."

Maybe Matthew 5:11 goes more appropriately with Matthew 5:13-16, and maybe there is a very important reason behind it. Perhaps Jesus was calling here for followers to do more than merely add a rich spice to life and to preserve the highest standard of living within life. Persecution is sometimes the context within which Christians are called to be the "salt of the earth."

Jesus was warning those who sought to be his disciples that a life of real Christian witness does not come without paying a certain price. He wanted those would-be followers to realize that if Christian faith is genuinely expressed through people's lives, then they are likely to be ostracized by the world because of what they believe. Sometimes being a disciple means standing over against the status quo and standing up against the accepted mode of behavior.

Sometimes being a disciple means worshiping together with people with whom we do not ordinarily mix, building bridges of understanding and relationship with others of God's children, and walking across those bridges of common faith in the Lordship of

Jesus Christ and of commitment to community to cooperate with God and with one another in loving the needy and dying world for which our Savior gave his very life.

Sometimes being a disciple of Jesus Christ means not just singing, "Jesus loves the little children of the world. Red and yellow, black and white, they are precious in his sight" but ACTING as though we really believe that truth. Sometimes it means moving beyond "talking the talk" to "walking the walk" of faith together as God's people. Sometimes being a disciple of Jesus Christ does mean standing over against the status quo and standing up against the accepted mode of behavior.

Salt is an ionic solid substance. It is able to withstand great heat without decomposing. Now it seems clear why Jesus referred to his most devoted disciples as the "salt of the earth."

In first-century Palestine brick ovens were kept outside peoples' homes. To insure that there would be a cooking fire the next morning, folk cut troughs in the bottoms of the ovens and poured in layers of salt. The salt acted like a catalyst. It maintained the heat level in the coals that were spread over the top of the salt. Thus, after the fire had burned down for the evening and was banked for the night, the salt below kept the heat. Then the next morning the oven temperature could be built up again.

Everybody knew that salt could take the heat. For that reason everybody knew exactly what Jesus meant when he called disciples to be like salt. Persecution is often the context within which we are called to be the "salt of the earth." "Salty Christians" are those who can stand the heat of a particular situation without decomposing in the process.

In the movie version of Harper Lee's novel *To Kill a Mockingbird*, Atticus Finch is a lawyer in a small Southern town. He is asked to defend a young black man who has been charged with attacking a white girl. He accepts the case, and overnight becomes the recipient of the abuse, scorn, and hatred of the people in the town. They become prejudiced against him as they are against the young defendant.

Atticus Finch holds his ground, despite all the local protest. The young black man is really innocent, and Finch defends him admirably. But, to no one's surprise, the jury hands over a guilty verdict.

Atticus Finch's two children come to the courthouse to watch their dad in action. Because they cannot find seats at the lower level, they go up to the balcony that is segregated and reserved for all the black people. There they sit down next to the town's black minister.

As the judge retires and various people start to leave the courtroom, Atticus Finch's daughter, Jean, is deep in thought and concentration, watching her dad and thinking about what he has just done. He stands all alone in the room, both actually and figuratively, putting his papers from the top of the table into his briefcase.

After slipping on his coat he walks down the aisle toward the exit, a man beaten by the jury's decision but a man with his soul still intact. He has withstood the rage of the population's prejudice and has lived through it without compromising his integrity or shortchanging his witness. He has taken the heat, and at the same time he has kept the faith.

Jean is engrossed to such an extent in watching her dad that she hardly notices someone has touched her on the shoulder. She turns around and notices that every black person in the balcony is standing. The black minister nudges her again, finally saying to her, "Miss Jean, stand up, your father is passing by."

No wonder they stood up. Atticus Finch was a man who could face persecution without giving up what he believed. He was a man who followed Jesus, not just to the foot of the cross, but also to the front of the courtroom.

Now there's a man who is really worth his salt. God help us to be just like him!

†††

What is God Doing in the Storm?

Mark 4:35–41; 6:45–51

Gerald L. Borchert

There are many designations for the contemporary world. They include the era of technology, nuclear fission, microcomputers, space travel communications, microsurgery and transplants. All indicate how far we have come in handling the world. According to the command in Genesis 1:28, we have indeed been fruitful. We have multiplied, filled the earth and subdued it, and have experienced dominion over the created order.

But that evaluation needs to be tempered by the fact that our world is filled with storms, with pain and with various forms of confusion. Many experience the effects of tornados, hurricanes, earthquakes, and wars, and we can even call a war a storm—a Desert Storm! We watch painfully the effects of over-population, the misuse of our environment and the lack of just means in the distribution of the world's resources so that many starve while others waste precious commodities necessary for life. To make matters worse we really do not know what to do with category four and five storms. We wait helplessly as we are broken to pieces by such forces in nature.

So for all our technological advance the question haunts us: How far have we really come beyond the Bible times and the real control of chaos? These facts have led me to read again the biblical stories of the creation and the sea, the flood and Noah, Jonah and the storm, Paul and the storm on the way to Rome, and Jesus and the stormy sea of Galilee.

I recalled again that the ancients gave names to the stormy seas. They called the sea *Tiamat*. In Acts 27:14 they called the storm *Eurakulo* (not merely "northeastern" as in some versions). The stormy seas between Italy and Sicily they called Cyclops. We have come a long way since that time, or have we? We can certainly fly in the eye of hurricanes; yet in spite of our sophistication, we still give storms names like Andrew, Iniki, and a host of other personal designations. Why? They are not just numbers; they seem to take on a life of their own.

Well, is there a message for the church in the storm? Is there a word to proclaim in the midst of chaos? I think there is. But the answer to chaos is not really in human power or ingenuity. There are, I believe, some clues in the storm stories of Jesus in Mark.

In Mark 4:38 Jesus lay sleeping in the boat, peacefully sleeping! The disciples, however, were terrified. The storm was almost swamping the boat. But Jesus was sleeping!

In Mark 6:45 the disciples were on the sea by themselves in a storm. They were in grave danger and they were able to make no progress in rowing to the shore. In the midst of the storm, Jesus came walking nonchalantly on the water. It was as though he was taking an early morning stroll. He did not even seem to notice the terrified disciples. Indeed, he was ready to pass them by.

In both stories the sea seemed to be roaring, roaring as it says in the Psalms (cf. 46:3; 96:11) like a monster. Chaos was attacking the disciples with full force. But chaos seemed to have absolutely no effect upon Jesus!

Then notice the next stage in these stories. In both stories there is a *terrified cry* for help by the disciples. "Don't you care that we are going to die?" "Are you so unconcerned that you would pass us by?" "What are you doing sleeping?"

That stage is followed by a strange sense of security on the part of Jesus in both stories. And there is a word of assurance. "Do not be afraid!" "Do not worry!"

But in both stories there is a strange twist. It is very strange. But it is surely the basis of a message for us today. In the first story Jesus was awakened by the disciples, arose, turned to the storm and said: "SHUT UP!" The translation in the KJV "Peace be still" just does not catch the meaning. When Jesus said "Shut up!" or "be muzzled" the storm immediately stopped blowing.

In the second story the ghost-like figure of Jesus was walking and when he heard the cries of the disciples he turned away from his morning stroll and climbed into the boat. Immediately the storm stopped.

In both cases the storm ceased but where is the twist? In both stories the twist is that the disciples who called for help in panic were totally stunned by the acts of Jesus. They were so stunned by the help that they really did not know how to handle it. Accordingly, they started to ask: "Who is this strange guy?" "He is really spooky!"

In seminary we give such spookiness a Latin name. We call it "the *mysterium tremendum.*" That really explains Jesus, or does it? It certainly sounds as though we know what we are talking about, or does it? But I wonder. I think it is just like when we start talking about God and say that God is immortal, invisible, omnipotent, omnipresent, and omniscient. Wow! We really are profound, or are we? I think I prefer the disciples thoughts: "Who is this strange guy?" "Don't you think he is spooky?"

For all our talk about God and Jesus we really do not understand God. When we speak in this manner we are saying that God is "In-" or "Im-" something. That means that God is "not" something. Or, God is "omni-," which means God is "all" something. Thus, God is either not or all something. Accordingly, what we have said in fact is that God is different than us. That is a magnificent revelation, or is it?

But where is the meaning of these storm stories for us? It is precisely at this point. We encounter all types of storms in our lives, in our homes, in our work, in our schools, and in our churches. They threaten us with chaos! They threaten our prosperity, our health, our families, and the very purpose and meaning of our lives. In helplessness we cry out to God. "Don't you care for us?" "Are you asleep?" "Are you going to pass us by?" "We are sinking and you seem to be sleeping?" "You are out for a walk!"

But we desperately hope that God knows that this life is not some Garden of Eden where God goes for a stroll. This life is chaos! And we continue to ask: "God, do you know the difference between a garden and chaos?" And God says: "I certainly do!" "But if I act, are you sure you can handle my action?"

The disciples for all their knowledge of Jesus had trouble understanding the way he acted. Will it be any different for us?

Are we ready for God to act in our chaos? Are you ready? Or do you only want God to act according to your prescriptions for God. Must God act the way we think God should act?

And what if God's action in your life seems to be inaction in the midst of chaos. That is the story of Job. God acts and God speaks in the storm but it may not be according to our wishes or our prayers.

God will certainly not be put in a test tube for us to play our game of divine existence. But you can be sure that God will act!

Yet chaos often seems to triumph in our homes and our churches. Bills pile up, people misuse us, illness strikes. These things happens because chaos is real. So we often cry out "let this cup pass from me!" (cf. Mark 14:36) And the answer often comes back, "Not now!" Even Jesus realized the force of chaos and cried out in forsakenness and anguish (cf. Mark 15:35). It all seemed lost. The storm seemed to win when Jesus was on the cross.

But the crucifixion was not the end of the story! One act of God has forever made it clear that God is present in the storm. That indelible act in history is the resurrection of Jesus Christ!

That act points all of us who believe beyond the pessimism of the storm to the only source that can give us hope in the midst of chaos. Genuine faith relies on God in the storm—even when the ship seems to be going under, when everything seems to be collapsing, when you watch a loved one suffer, and when all the world loses hope.

There is no doubt that chaos is real! But chaos could not entomb the God of the resurrection. And it was the resurrection of Jesus that changed terrified disciples from a boat into people who would face death for the sake of the gospel.

The question then is not whether you go to church, teach a Sunday school class, or even witness to your neighbor. *But the question is:* Can you live in the storm and go to church, teach Sunday school and witness to your neighbor! To live in the storm and discover God in that storm is the basis of a powerful life. That type of powerful living is the real message of the gospel.

Jesus is not merely calling us to be fair-weather Christians, rice Christians, or fairy-tale Christians who think everything ends happily ever after. Jesus is calling us to join him in the storm and discover the serenity of God's touch on us when chaos is ripping at the very order of our lives. The invitation comes to each of us. Are you willing to join the Lord in the storm?

Remember: "God is our refuge and strength, a very present help in trouble" (Ps 46:1).

†††

Reverence, Revision, and Redeeming Love

Acts 13:13-41

Linda McKinnish Bridges

It was 1979, and political relations between the United States and Taiwan, Republic of China had abruptly ended.[1] In order to establish relationships with Mainland China, American ties to Taiwan had to be dissolved. We were there, living in the capital city of Taipei. Hostility against America and U.S. citizens began to boil on the streets of the city. Some Americans were seriously injured. Anger resulted in street demonstrations, rock throwing and protests. The embassy advised all U.S. citizens to remain in their houses for safety until further notice. We began to plan our weekend at home. And then I remembered.

I had promised to meet Lyou Ji, a young seminary student, at the chapel for visitation. "Surely, he'll understand why I'm not there," I thought. The more comfortable I tried to be at home, the more restless I became. I felt that I should go on to the church, but I was afraid to leave our apartment. I thought of my friend, Lyou Ji, quietly sitting in the front room of the old apartment building-turned-church waiting for me to arrive. I decided that I needed to go—that I had to go.

I nervously got into my car, rolled up my coat collar, pulled down my cap over my eyes, dropped down in the seat, and drove the thirty minutes across town.

"So far, so good, no one recognized me," I thought. As I drove, I created a new visitation plan as I listened for a news update on the military radio station. Not one looking for missionary martyrdom, I devised a clever alternative. "When I get to the chapel, this is what I'll do," I thought to myself. "I will pray with Lyou Ji, and then stay in the chapel while he, alone, will walk through the village meeting people and having supper at the open air noodle stand. I will be safe there in the apartment and, of course, in prayer for him." Sounded like a good plan to me.

When I arrived, we greeted one another, and discussed the political tension between our two countries. I then proposed what I thought the ideal visitation plan. "You go on," I said. "I'll stay here safe in the chapel and do my part by being in prayer for you here."

Lyou Ji made no response. Then this young, quiet, Chinese seminary student, who had never, ever corrected me not even when my language was painfully incorrect, began to teach me an important lesson about the gospel of Jesus Christ.

Meek, unassuming Lyou Ji looked at me and said, "Bwo shr mu, you are a citizen from the country of the United States, right? And it is a good place with fine people. And you should be proud of your citizenship."

I said, "Yes, Lyou Ji, I am."

He continued, "Bwo shr mu, you are also a Christian, right? And being a Christian means that you have another citizenship, that you also belong to God's kingdom as well as to America. Right?"

I said, "Yes, Lyou Ji, of course, that is why I am here."

"Well, Bwo shr mu, it seems to me that since you are also a citizen of God's kingdom, then you can go out tonight not simply representing the kingdom of America but representing your other citizenship—God's kingdom."

"What do you mean, Lyou Ji?" I replied. Then, in a moment of painful revelation, I said, "Oh, I am afraid that I see what you mean." I heard him, oh boy, did I hear. My heart and mind were pricked to the quick.

"You are absolutely right, Lyou Ji. That's it, Lyou Ji. Let me get my coat. Let's go."

We walked out together. Oh, I still had my collar up and my hat down. I still looked carefully, all the while making possible escape plans when I saw large groups of people coming in my direction. I still was a little nervous eating noodles in the open air market. But Lyou Ji and I were together doing the work of the church.

I had taken courses in missiology; I had the prerequisite missionary training experience. I knew the theories of trans-culturalization. But that night I learned something about the nature of the gospel and my responsibility to it from a quiet, unassuming Chinese young man who was, underneath his humility and slight, physical posture, a theological giant.

I learned that I could not deny that I was an American. I looked it. I thought like an American. I acted like an American. And that being an American was good. Lyou Ji, however, so gently reminded me that my identity as a child of God took precedence over any cultural identity that I may have proposed. Revising my understanding of citizenship became prerequisite to my relationship to the Chinese people.

Paul understood it. Paul knew that he was a Jew. He looked like a Jew. He studied as a Jew. He thought like a Jew. He also knew somehow that the gospel was something more than Jewish thought customs. And that was revolutionary! How then did this radical gospel take root in such Jewish soil? How did the revolution take place?

Successful revolutions of any kind must keep the delicate balance between deep reverence for the past and a radical revision of the present. Alfred North Whitehead says that "those societies that cannot combine reverence for their symbols with freedom of revision must ultimately decay from anarchy or slow atrophy."[2] The planting of the gospel in the first-century soil demanded a delicate balance between reverence for the past and revision for the present.

Paul's sermon in the synagogue in Antioch of Pisidia gives us a telescopic view of the balance between reverence and revision. Paul has been commissioned by the church in Antioch of Syria. From there he goes to Seleucia, then to Cyprus, then to Antioch of Pisidia. By now, Paul has crossed over one third of Asia Minor.

The plot of Luke's story intensifies. Paul arrives in town, and, as was his custom, finds the synagogue. He is asked to speak. He tells a familiar story. He had heard the story before as a young boy in Hebrew school. He had recited it time and time again as a young adult at the Passover table. And once again, with a deep sense of reverence, he recites the sacred history:

"You Israelites and you that fear God, listen: The God of this people Israel chose our ancestors and made the people great during their stay in the land of Egypt, and with uplifted arm he led them out of it. Remember the forty years in the wilderness? Remember Samuel? Remember Saul? And remember David?"

The listeners smile, for they, too, know the sacred stories. They are proud to hear them once again. It reminds them of their heritage and the faithfulness of God in their midst. They begin to question why Paul has received such bad press as a radical rebel.

And then it happens. The scene changes. The course of history changes. The old familiar story now sounds different. Paul adds a new chapter. Paul continues to say,

> And from David's posterity God has brought to Israel a Savior, Jesus, as he promised. . . . whom the leaders in Jerusalem killed, because they did not recognize him even while they were reading the scriptures every Sabbath in the synagogue. But God raised him from the dead. . . . Let it be known that through this one forgiveness of sins is proclaimed to you.

Paul has now revised the familiar story line replacing the usual conclusion with a radically different ending—one that introduces a new Savior, Jesus Christ. The listener is caught off guard. "This is new; we want to hear more on the next Sabbath," the people exclaim.

The next Sabbath came and the whole city was there, as well as some angry traditionalists. When they saw that Jews and Gentiles were present, they were hostile. It was one thing to deconstruct the tradition orally, it is another thing to demolish it totally by allowing the common people—the gentiles—to respond. Paul and Barnabas, however, were not silenced by the angry mob. Their mission was to redeem people not to perpetuate religious structures. And they continued. And as the conclusion of the passage states,". . . the word of the Lord spread throughout the region" (13:49).

How did they do it? Paul had experienced the Risen Lord. He had known Yahweh in the past, and now he knew Christ. He had respect for the former traditions, yet he knew that the demands of the gospel were so great that revision of the past was inevitable.

Circumcision was okay as a tradition; but don't expect it to bring salvation, the revisionist Paul said. Paul continued, the Law was important as a teacher/custodian; but don't expect it to bring redemption. In Paul's understanding of the gospel, a healthy view of his past remained. He was able to appropriate the traditions of his past into the radical gospel, except one, a very important one. In Paul's new understanding of faith, one tradition had to be totally eradicated—barriers between people, the Jews and Gentiles.

Some of the listeners understood that Jesus the Messiah was God, that was no major problem. But the greatest hurdle for those listening in the synagogue on the second Sabbath was that this new story had a sociological and theological purpose. The Gospel was for people and included both groups—Jews and Gentiles. Paul did not plan it that way. He did not set out to include Gentiles any more than he determined to kill Christians in his former life. He did not write the gospel; he only lived it. And where it went it meant that Gentiles were also to be included, regardless of the past social codes of the Jewish world. Paul's vision of the gospel maintained a reverence for the tradition, all the while fearlessly, even ruthlessly at times, revising it.

As he traveled it became clear. The gospel message came from the delicate balance of reverence, revision, and redeeming love. The result of his commitment to the message of Jesus Christ was that the gospel was universal, for everyone. Intrinsic to the life of this missionary was not simply geographical expansion nor doctrinal purity. The force of the gospel energized traditional Jews to sit at table with common Gentiles. And that was radical. It was for the sake of redeeming love that Paul started out in the first place—redeeming love between God and God's people, between Jews and Gentiles, male and female, slave and free. Love for people, wherever they were and whoever they were, became the energizing force behind this missionary giant and his mission.

And so here we are as Baptists, whose essence of being is mission. But, as you know, we are caught in the delicate balance of being somewhere back there in time and somewhere out there in the future. But if we are to move ahead, we first move by looking back with reverence and thanksgiving, not anger or bitterness. We do have a history of missions to remember. Our sacred stories of the past invoke memories of people like Lottie Moon, who although Virginian became Chinese for the sake of the gospel. We have others—of Sunbeams, of RA's, of Baker James Cauthen, of powerful missions sermons and appointment services on hot June evenings in huge convention centers, of Annie Armstrong, of new churches in New England, of downtown mission centers in New Orleans, of Alma Hunt, of feeding the hungry in Ethiopia, of outside services in Chinese peasant huts, of teaching children of native Americans in Oklahoma, of giving bread and drink from the table of your own home, and on and on the story goes on. It is a good story, one to be remembered and cherished, but we cannot stop there.

For there are those of us who are in the process of revising this special tradition—revising it so that women's voices can be heard in Baptist pulpits across our land proclaiming the missionary message; revising it so that the faithful women who raise the mission money can also decide how to spend it; revising it so that the voice of the little church can be heard side by side with the voice of the big church; revising it so that laypeople are not considered second-class citizens in God's work. WE ARE NOT AFRAID OF REVISION. We are moving out in new avenues of missiological thinking, not taking Christ TO but being IN Christ WITH; constantly exploring new ways to meet the needs of the growing poor in our country, of the unreached people groups of other countries, dreaming new ways of doing old things, like theological education for the purpose of building and strengthening churches. We are not afraid of the new because like Paul and his gospel we have a rich, rich heritage that has strengthened our understanding of God and God's relationships with people.

But we have also learned that the connecting link in this delicate balance between reverence and revision is not for the sake of the denominational structure, not for the purpose of maintaining the bureaucracy, not even for the purpose of maintaining strict orthodoxy and pure dogma. These things fade and change with time. But our focus is on people—a genuine concern for people, wherever they are in their journey. Concern for people becomes the connecting link.

We continue the task of mission because we are committed to people. Because we still believe that the world needs Jesus Christ. Because we still believe that the primary purpose of the gospel is to bring people into relationship with Jesus Christ. Our message is carved out of reverence for our former tradition, with a radical commitment to revision, energized by God's redeeming love. Thank you, Lyou Ji, for you taught me a great deal on that eventful evening.

In my North Carolina mountain tradition we still sing it this way: E'er since by faith I saw the stream/Thy flowing wounds supply,/Redeeming love has been my theme,/And shall be till I die:/And shall be till I die,/And shall be till I die;/Redeeming love has been my theme,/And shall be till I die.

Amen. God bless you.

Notes

[1]This sermon was first preached May 1, 1992 at the General Assembly of the Cooperative Baptist Fellowship in Fort Worth, Texas.

[2]Alfred North Whitehead. *Symbolism: Its Meaning and Effect* (New York: Macmillan, 1927) 88.

✝✝✝

Discipleship:
A Markan Perspective

Donald E. Cook

Analysis

The words *disciple* and *discipleship* are fascinating. We may use them in a variety of ways in English to express a certain understanding of the beginning and/or development of faith. Some may use the verb to speak of a person's being *discipled,* that is evangelized, while the adjective in a phrase such as *discipleship training* suggests educating believers in the meaning and practice of their commitment to the Lord. Furthermore, we employ the noun *disciple* not only to refer to a member of Jesus' original band, but to any person who follows the Lord. Somehow the words relate simultaneously to the beginning and development of faith and to ancient and modern experience. They seem to bridge the gap between then and now and require that we face the ancient demands of Christ in our contemporary world both as decision and as a way of life.

For these reasons it is legitimate, I think, to ask you to reflect with me upon the meaning of discipleship in light of our Lord's call of his disciples.

Mark wrote his Gospel in the 60s or 70s of the first century to proclaim that the man on the cross is Messiah and Son of God. Mark's narrative was carefully conceived and executed by one who was both a literary artist and a theological genius. The first evangelist was a person of deep faith who put his considerable talents to work to create a new literary form—a story to proclaim the good news, a Gospel.

Most students of Mark's Gospel sense that the work is divided into two parts, with the confession of Peter at Caesarea (8:29) serving as the climax of the first half and the beginning of the second. In 1:1 Mark tells us who Jesus is: Christ and Son of God, a theme that is reflected and refracted at baptism (1:11), through Peter's confession (8:29), in transfiguration (9:7) and at crucifixion (15:39). Further, it is generally agreed that upon Peter's confession there is initiated a series of three passion saying cycles (8:31-9:1; 9:30-50; 10:32-45) which, beginning at Caesarea, punctuate Jesus' journey to his cross at Jerusalem.

On this occasion we shall consider mainly certain events prior to Caesarea in an effort to reclaim, if we can, a sub-theme of the narratives by which Mark sought to confront and involve his church in discipleship—the calling of the disciples of Jesus. I take the narrative of the call of the first disciples in a parabolic sense, demanding response to the Living Lord. This is not a denial of their basic historicity, but an understanding of the passages as an appeal beyond history by means of *his story.* I think that this is the way in which Mark intended his gospel to be heard/read.

According to Mark, Jesus did three things following his baptism by John and his temptation: he went to Galilee, he preached, he called his first disciples. The alert reader will note that, after the first calling, events do not occur helter-skelter, but in a relatively ordered pattern of what appear to be cycles[1], each beginning with a call to the disciples and ending with some form of rejection. Although we would not wish to impose a rigid format on the narrative, it is quite possible to outline the first half of the gospel in this manner, with the fourth and final cycle overflowing into the Caesarea confession complex and ending with Peter's rejection of Jesus' decision to go to the cross. This rejection, moreover, is the background for a new kind of discipleship saying addressed both to the multitude and to the disciples—the demand for cross bearing. We shall come back to this saying at the end of the message. At the moment, however, we must consider the importance our evangelist attaches to the calling of the disciples. This importance is attested by:

(1) The placement of the first call at the beginning of Jesus' public ministry.
(2) The repetition of the call motif in what appears to be a progressive sequence throughout the first half of the gospel.
(3) The use of a common vocabulary and similar literary form in the callings.

Now let us look at each of the calling passages and attempt to interpret them.

The Call of the Four

> And passing along by the Sea of Galilee, he saw Simon and Andrew the brother of Simon casting a net in the sea; for they were fishermen. And Jesus said to them, "Follow me and I will make you become fishers of men." And immediately they left their nets and followed him. And going on a little farther, he saw James the son of Zebedee and John his brother, who were in their boat mending their nets. And immediately he called them; and they left their father Zebedee in the boat with the hired servants, and followed him (1:16-20, RSV).[2]

In the call of the first disciples, Jesus saw the brothers at their honest work (cf. 1 Sam 16:7 where God saw David as king before Samuel anointed him). This seeing issues in call. Note the divine authority of Jesus in the elective act and the unhesitating response of the brothers to abandon all and follow Jesus. By the time Mark wrote, "following" was already a technical expression for discipleship. These elements of divine initiative and human faith-response are basic to each development of Mark's narrative presentation of discipleship. The figure "make you fishers of men" draws upon the circumstances of call in this narrative and anticipates the appointment and mission of the twelve in 3:14-19 and 6:7-13. Mark's hand is clearly seen by the double use of "immediately" (*euthys*).

The Call of Levi

> And as he passed on, he saw Levi the son of Alphaeus sitting at the tax office, and he said to him, "Follow me." And he rose and followed him (2:14).

> "I came not to call the righteous, but sinners" (2:17).

The question of the precise identity of Levi vexes the interpretation of this passage and will not be settled here. In my judgment, however, the tax collector ought to be identified with Matthew (3:18; cf. Matt 9:9). The paramount concern for our evangelist, however, is not that problem of synoptic criticism, but the astounding act that Jesus saw (Note that word!) Levi in the act of doing his dirty work and summoned the outcast to follow him. And Levi did, just as the four had done before him. This pericope builds upon the earlier call narrative to show us that the call of Jesus is not only an initiative of divine authority, but an act of grace to which even an outcast can respond. The following story of the dinner attended by "many tax collectors and sinners" makes this point abundantly clear with the saying of Jesus: "I came not to call the righteous, but sinners" (2:17).

The Call and Appointment of the Twelve

> And he went up into the hills, and called to him those whom he desired; and they came to him. And he appointed twelve, to be with him, and to be sent out to preach and have authority to cast out demons: Simon whom he surnamed Peter; James the son of Zebedee. . . (3:13-17).

The third calling account functions as a summation and elaboration of the two previous passages and prepares the way for a fourth. It is a precisely written descriptive narrative, considerably more detailed than the parallel passages in Matthew 10:1-4 and Luke 6:12-16. Such care in composition is a further indication of the importance our evangelist attached to this dimension of Jesus' activity.

The reference to "the hills" (Greek, "the mountain") probably is a reflection of the Old Testament tradition associating mountain with he giving and receiving of divine revelation (cf. Exod 19:20; 1 Kgs 19:8; Matt 5:1; cf. Mark 9:2).

Again the calling motif centers about divine sovereignty and initiative, although greatly intensified. He "called to him those whom he desired" (literally, "willed" [*ēthelen*]). The response, also, is the same as earlier: "They came to him." The appointment of the twelve may be seen as the result of the selection process considered earlier. It is parallel to Jesus' calling "whom he desired." In this connection, it should be noted that the verb "appoint" here and the verb "make" in the "fishers of men" figure (1:17) translate the same Greek term (*poieō*). The persons previously called (except, of course, Levi, unless Levi = Matthew) are included in the number twelve, which probably is a symbolic reference to the twelve tribes (possibly a New Israel motif, cf. Matt 19:28; Luke 22:30). (The phrase "whom he names apostles," though fairly well supported in the manuscript evidence, is probably an assimilation from Luke 6:13 and will not be discussed here.)

The purpose (*hina*) of the call of the twelve now comes to the fore: "to be with him and to be sent out" (*apostellō*). (The grammar is clearer in Greek than in English.) Being with Jesus suggest fellowship with the Master and learning from him first hand. They are to see his deeds and hear his words—they will become eyewitnesses (cf. Acts 1:21; Luke 1:1-2).

Note further that just as Jesus called the twelve, so it is Jesus who sends them out. Their being sent is predicated upon their being with the Master. The twelve are commissioned "to preach and to have authority to cast out demons." These are messianic tasks. The disciples are to announce the good news of God's Reign and to demonstrate the coming of Messiah by asserting his authority over the powers of evil. In short, they are to take up the tasks that Jesus began in the world.

Significantly, only after their tasks were assigned were their names mentioned.

The Sending Out of the Twelve

And he called to him the twelve, and began to send them out two by two, and gave them the authority over the unclean spirits. He charged them to take nothing for their journey except a staff; . . . So they went out and preached that men should repent. And they case out many demons, and anointed with oil many that were sick and healed them (6:7-8, 12-13).

The apostles returned to Jesus, and told him all that they had done and taught (6:30).

The fourth calling passage completes the third by making explicit the tasks of the twelve. They are sent out in pairs with messianic authority, and nothing else! Their message (repentance) is almost identical to that of Jesus' first preaching (1:14-15) and, their mighty works of exorcism and healing are extensions of the Master's deeds. They are representatives of the Christ. It is not surprising, then, that when the twelve return from their mission—now described further in terms of teaching—Mark designates them "apostles"—those who were sent out.

Application

Now that we have seen something of what Mark was saying to his church about discipleship (and we must admit that we have touched only a small portion of what he was saying), our second task remains: What do these texts say to us? Does God have a Word for us in this scripture?

It is quite fitting that we should discuss calling and discipleship together. By means of his developing narrative, Mark has much to say to us on discipleship and ministry in our world. Let me share with you what I see here. You may see more or less.

(1) The call of Jesus is always at his initiative. Mark portrays a quality of sovereign authority about Jesus that is irreducibly divine. The call of Jesus is the call of God.

In light of the teaching of Mark's gospel, it seems strange that throughout the history of the church, and even in our own day, there have been those who, in the name of whatever gods they serve, challenge the right of Jesus Christ to call whomever he will. In my reading of the Marcan text, I find no test for calling—sexual, racial, educational, doctrinal, whatever—save the word of Jesus in grace.

(2) The call of Jesus is a call to followship and fellowship. "Follow me" (1:17) is an intensely personal invitation and being "with him" (3:14) is an almost ineffable descriptive. These are the qualities which Mark sees as foundational to being made "fishers of men" (1:17) and being "sent out" (3:14). Mark has brought us to that same sense of immediacy, that same relational source of life

and power that we encounter in Paul's "in Christ" and in that marvelous Johannine phrase "which we have seen with our eyes, which we have looked upon and touched with our hands" (1 John 1:1). In the call and in its subsequent development in life, Jesus comes to us and summons us to be with him. Personal encounter with the Risen Lord is the only authentication of discipleship and, ultimately, the only empowering of Christian witness in the world.

(3) The call of Jesus demands obedience: They or he "followed him" (1:18; 20; 2:14); "They came to him" (3:13); "they went out" (6:12). The sequence of these phrases is not accidental. It traces a development of response. Proper discipleship begins and ends in faith-obedience. Mark's assertion is made even more forceful by the counter-point of the disciples' dullness and lack of faith elsewhere in the Gospel (8:14-21; 10:32-45; 14:50).

The call to preach, teach, heal, and confront the demons of the world is a call to take up the task begun by Jesus. We live in an apocalyptic age teetering on the edge of disaster. There are many voices, many shouts, but only one call—the call of the Risen Lord.

> Come, follow me
>   to places dark with fear and sin,
>   to islands of despair and mountains of loneliness,
>   across deserts hot with the hatred of unloved masses
>   and frosty with the chill of abandoned hopes without
>   and within,
>   to the reaches of the universe, wherever human kind may be
>   and give them love found only in a cross.

Indeed, the cross seems to be the key to discipleship in Mark, as it is for messiahship. And it is through the cross that Mark enlarges his calling motif to include all Christians.

Let's return to his story one more time:

Discipleship and a Cross

Mark's standard for discipleship is utter self denial—a cross. There have been foreshadowings of this earlier: The brother "left their nets" (1:18); "They left their father" (1:20). Levi left his tax table (2:14). Our evangelist has structured his narrative so that the supreme discipleship saying of Jesus stands apart from the calling of the twelve yet is clearly related to those events, interpreting them. It comes immediately following Peter's rejection of Jesus' intention to go to Jerusalem to die, (8:32) and is addressed not to the disciples alone, but to all those about Jesus: ". . . he called to him the multitude with his disciples" (8:34). The passage is loaded with the vocabulary of the previous callings and continues their form, but for the first time the call is conditional, yet universal:

> If anyone wishes to come after me,
>   let him/her deny self,
>   take up his cross,
>   and follow me. (8:34)[3]

Brothers and sisters, that extends the call and a cross to each of us and all of us. Discipleship is learned at the cross or not at all.

> He calls;
> I follow.
> He teaches;
> I learn.
> He sends;
> I go.
> I am His;
> He is mine,
> My Lord, divine.

Notes

[1]1:16-2:12; 2:13-3:12; 3:13-6:6; 6:7-8:33. Cf. E. Schweizer, "The Portrayal of the Life of Faith in the Gospel of Mark," *Interpreting the Gospels*, James Luther Mays, ed. (Philadelphia: Fortress Press, 1981) 168-82.

[2]All scripture quotations in this sermon are from the RSV, (1952), unless otherwise noted.

[3]My paraphrase is based on Nestle-Aland, 26th ed.

†††

A Standing Exam for Servants of God

1 Thessalonians 1-2

Bruce Corley

In 1 Thessalonians, chapters 1-2, there is a stirring description of a revival. Open your Bible to these two chapters, because I put them before you as the text for this sermon. These chapters have an unusual concentration of the word for "becoming," an event, a happening. In the language of the King James Version, it is the phrase often translated "it came to pass."

This "happening" at Thessalonica is described in ten different ways. Note them in order, beginning with, the gospel *became* (1:5). It *came* with power, the Holy Spirit, and a full conviction on the part of the preachers. Then again, the preachers *became* (1:5). Their conduct was known by the Thessalonians. Finally, the hearers *became* imitators (1:7). They *became* types for others. The next chapter centers on Paul and the church. Paul's entrance did not *become* empty (2:1). Neither did his preaching *come* with flattering words (2:5). He *became* gentle toward them (2:7), and they became beloved to him (2:8). He *became* admirable in their eyes, having led a blameless life (2:10). They *became* imitators of suffering churches (2:14). Ten uses of the same verb (Greek *genesthai*, to become)!

It refers to a threefold happening in, for want of a better word, a "revival," or perhaps one of our words that is closer to the New Testament, "evangelism." The first is the becoming of the *word*, the power of the gospel proclaimed. Then there is the becoming of *believers* in Jesus Christ; they are transformed, and their lives give evidence of it. Lastly, there is the becoming of the *messengers*, the heralds of the saving word. The evangel—the gospel, the evangelized—those who believe, and the evangelists—the heralds of God, they are marked by a "becoming." Therein lies my interest, my text, and my sermon. Not the powerful gospel, although the idea is so attractive, not transformed believers, but the kind of people who herald the gospel.

I direct your attention to two phrases in the passage that draw together what I will say. The first, 2:4, is translated in the New International Version, "God who tests our hearts." Howard Marshall put it this way: "God's scrutiny is not, as it were, a once-for-all entrance examination for his servants but a continually operative process of what might nowadays be called 'quality-control'."[1] It is a standing examination. God tests the hearts of those who would be his servants. Around graduate schools one should not tell people what the question is on the standing exam. I am going to tell you the question, and, believe it or not, I am going to give you the answers to the exam. It is not hard to find the answers; they are simply hard to live up to.

The second word is a very small pronoun found in 1:5 and translated in the New International Version, "how we lived among you." The King James Version says, "what manner of"; others translate it, "what kind of people." I suggest that we find two ideas in this pronoun: *Who* we *are* and *what* we *do*. Or, to turn it into my question for this exam, What kind of people should the servants of God be? That is the question. Let me suggest the answers that Paul would give to that question around three headings.

I. Answer One:
The servants of God must be trustworthy.

In 2:4 Paul states the heart of being God's servant: "We are approved by God to be entrusted with the gospel." Paul would not separate his ministry and his message from himself. In the marketplaces of the ancient cities there were unending varieties of super-slick salesmen: religious charlatans who talked smooth things about religion, flim-flam artists, con men, those who used the power of words to deceive and to exploit their hearers. Paul did not cut corners and bring his message into disrepute by that kind of mass-market appeal. His denials of unwholesome motives have a staccato effect: no falsehood, no moral impurity, no trickery, no flattery, no coverups to exploit people, no menpleasing speeches. We might paraphrase his attitude as never "playing to the galleries," that is, saying the things that they want you to say in order for you to gain a hearing.

We are entrusted with a divine word, not a human word. How we speak, the style of the appeal, is a keen measure of trustworthiness. A lot of things heard nowadays sound like they come from the Joe Isuzu School of Bible. I have concocted an excerpt, it goes like this:

> There was a son of the Pharisees named Nicodemus, the same came to Jericho by night and fell among thorns. And the thorns grew up and choked him, leaving him half dead. And by chance there came down Solomon and his wife Gomorrah, and they made for him an ark of bulrushes and daubed him with slime and with pitch. And the Pharaoh stood afar off, to wit what would be done to him. No one could come nigh to him for the press, but three young men from the fiery furnace laid hold on him, and he left the linen cloth and fled from them naked. As he was running prodigal through the eastern gate, he went under the low limbs of a great oak, and his head caught hold of the oak. He hung there between the heavens and the earth forty days and forty nights. Being grievously tormented, he was afterward an hungered, and the ravens came and fed him. The three wise men from the east of Jerusalem came saying, "Will you rise up to flee?" And he went down to Joppa and found a ship going to Nineveh. When he entered the city a day's journey, he saw Jezebel looking out a window. She painted her face because she was tired of her head. And he said, "Chunk her down, boys!" And they answered, "How oft . . . till seven times?" He said, "I say not unto thee, seven times, but until seventy times seven." And they chunked her down 490 times. And falling headlong, she burst asunder in their midst. And they took up twelve baskets full of fragments. Then the prodigal son wanting the portion of goods that fell to him asked, "Therefore in the resurrection which one of these will be my wife?"

Heavenly word salad! Of course, I am being facetious, but there is an epidemic of crisis proportion in the media and pulpits of our country concerning our talk. Are we trustworthy? Are we credible? Are we honest? Would you prostitute the ministry—which is not yours, God has entrusted it to you—would you prostitute the ministry for your own ends? Remember that all of us are authorized, not authorities. Each servant has been entrusted, and he who entrusts can also take that trust away. What is the difference in a stem-winding, spell-binding preacher and a slick, snake-oil salesman? Trustworthiness. We need a revival of it. What should the servants of God be? Trustworthy.

II. The Second Answer:
The servants of God must be softhearted and caring.

I have chosen "softhearted" and "caring" to describe what is said in the sentence, "We are gentle among you like a mother caring for her little children" (2:7). How strange to hear an apostle talk this way. He concedes a heavy authority by saying, "We could have been weighty" (2:6). Paul loved a turn of phrase, and I can see the smile on his face when he said, "I could have leaned on you folks, but among you I was gentle as a mother nursing her baby." For Paul being an apostle meant being *fatherly*. In 2:11-12 he reminds them that he encouraged, comforted, and urged them as a father to his own children. But for Paul being an apostle also meant being *motherly*, caring for a baby, loving deeply, giving your soul for your child.

One of Paul's most astute commentators, Charles E. B. Cranfield, says of this passage: "Gentleness is an apostolic quality that is by no means common. . . . How many of the clergy would be more accurately described as inclined to be arrogant, self-willed, stubborn, domineering, than as gentle!"[2] Have we been taught to think that we have to be mean as the Devil and cold as ice to pastor a church so that we cannot care? Plastic professionals are deadly. We fool ourselves if we try to give people a message without giving them our souls.

Here is a good measure of how caring you are: Do babies cry and children run? If a preacher has kids that love him, anyone can love that preacher. In our world where the *sclerotic* (Greek "hard") pattern of ministry is so strong, we need the *apiotic* (Greek "gentle"); in Paul's world that is the way one distinguished in speech between "hard" people and "gentle" people. What should the servants of God be? They should be caring, softhearted.

III. Finally, Answer Three:
The servants of God must be exemplary.

"You became imitators of us and of the Lord" (1:6). The servants of God should become the model of Christianity, that is, serving as a pattern for others to follow. Paul says this six times (1 Cor 4:16; 11:1; Phil 3:17; 4:9; 1 Thess 1:6; 2 Thess 3:7, 9) in his writings: Imitate me as I imitate Christ. It is the audacity of a life that is worthy of the Lord, and as Dizzy Dean once said, "If it's true it ain't bragging!" We excuse ourselves by telling our people, "do as I say not as I do." Paul will have none of that. He tell his churches, "Whatever you have learned, or received or heard from me, or *seen in me*—put it into practice" (Phil 4:9). Mind you this, the models we follow are more important than all of the materials we master and the methods we learn. That is why some people never get hold of what Christianity is about. It is not a question of whether we have models (we do) or whether they are influential (they are); it is a question of the kind that we have. Every revival is a call to Christianity in action by example. There must be in the preacher the example of the life that the message gives.

Paul says in 2 Corinthians 6:3, that he is very careful not to put a stumbling block that will cause someone to find fault with the ministry. The word "to find fault, to discredit, to ridicule," recalls a God in the Greek pantheon name Momus. Momus was the God of ridicule. While Zeus ran around hurling thunderbolts at weaklings, threatening to send great floods in the earth, Momus sat to the side, laughing and ridiculing him because he could not handle his affairs. In fact, Momus suggested sarcastically to Zeus that the way to really trouble his disobedient creatures was to get them to fight with one another. Momus became a verb in the Greek language. It was handy for someone who sat to the side and laughed at those who messed up an important task. Paul was keenly aware of preserving the honor of the ministry by being exemplary for the people that he lived before. I call you to that. God expects no less than that in your life.

T. R. Glover, the famous classical scholar, former orator at the University of Cambridge, and Baptist deacon, described growth in Christ as the difference in a discovery and an exploration.[3] A discoverer says, "Come and see, look what I found." An explorer says, "Come and see, and follow me after it." Professor Glover tells the story of one of the most fascinating chapters in geography, the early exploration of America. The Chesapeake Bay was missed on several maps. Fog and darkness may have been the cause of the explorer missing the place, but he missed it. Glover proposes what might have happened when later explorers came. They were surprised in those early days, expecting nothing there, suddenly to come upon a body of water of great magnitude. What was it? The shore showed no break on the map. Here was a huge inlet, or was it an outlet? Was it the arm of a sea, a vast bay, a great river? A great deal depended on which it was, and there were several ways that the truth could be determined. One was to sail up and map it carefully. Of course, there was a quicker way: To drop a bucket over the side and draw up the water. That submerged bucket, being drawn up with fresh water, brought a moment of revelation in the tasting. The discovery was not a bay, not an inlet, but a great river. They discovered no island, no peninsula. The tasting of fresh water revealed a great continent to be explored.

People who are explorers in Jesus Christ are exemplary servants. They have tasted fresh water, and they pursue it inland. They have ceased dipping in the blush of discovery; they have gone on into him. They lead others by example to be explorers in Jesus Christ.

What kind of revival do we need? We need the kind that helps servants to pass God's standing exam. Trustworthy. Caring. Exemplary.

Notes

[1]I. Howard Marshall, *1-2 Thessalonians,* The New Century Bible (Grand Rapids: Eerdmans, 1983) 65-66.

[2]C. E. B. Cranfield, *The Bible and the Christian Life* (Edinburgh: T & T Clark, 1985) 30.

[3]T. R. Glover, *The Jesus of History* (London: SCM, 1917) 220-21.   †††

The Second Call,
the Second Baptism

Mark 10:35-45

R. Alan Culpepper

Let me invite you to take a trip in your imagination. I want you to imagine how you would live, if you could live any way you wanted to live. Imagine a life of ease, success, or achievement. For example, would you want the success and glamour of being president of a large, successful company? Would you want the leisure of a long, healthful retirement? Maybe you would want to travel to distant places or keep company with the rich and famous? Probably most of us have already begun to shape our lives in ways that begin to approximate the life of our dreams, but we can immediately think of ways that we would change our lives if we could.

I.

I suppose that is one reason I was attracted to a short story called "The Crumb" by a young writer named Sunny Rogers.[1] The other reason is that the lead character is named Haber Hill Culpepper. Haber Hill as his name suggests, lives a life of ease on a plantation in Virginia. He is a retired law professor who spends his days reading poetry, history, and philosophy, seeking some disclosure of the Divine. He is not a religious man but a reverent one. Each day he reads a passage of scripture, two poems, and passages of great literature. On one day, Haber Hill read a poem by Emily Dickinson:

> God gave a loaf to every Bird—
> But just a Crumb—to Me—
> I dare not eat it—tho' I starve—
> My poignant luxury. . . .

I wonder how the Rich—may feel—
An Indiaman—An Earl—
I deem that I—with but a Crumb—
Am Sovereign of them all.

II.

Let us leave Haber Hill for the time being as he searches for his disclosure of the Divine and remember James and John, the sons of Zebedee, who had embarked on their own journey of discovery. They had left their nets and their father in response to the call of Jesus. The Gospel of Mark chronicles a story of mixed success and failure. James and John were searching for their dreams too. In Jesus they saw someone who could make those dreams come true.

Before they met Jesus they had lived out lives of drudgery, rising early and working late. Stretching drag nets, and hauling them in, repairing the nets, sorting the catch, carrying it to the markets and processing plants, and then seeing up to thirty percent of their income go to taxes. (Some things don't change do they?) To make matters worse, they lived under the oppressive rule of the Roman Empire. Like other Galileans, James and John remembered the glory days when Israel had been a sovereign kingdom under God's rule and those he had appointed. They longed for the coming kingdom of God, when the Romans would be run out and God's blessing of Israel would be manifest to all the world.

If we asked the fishermen how they would want to live, they would have told us that they could think of nothing more wonderful than to have important places in the kingdom when once again glory was restored to Israel. For the two fisherman it must have seemed that there could never be any chance that their dreams would come true. Even if the kingdom were restored to Israel during their lifetimes, how could they ever expect to have places of power in it. Like Tevie in "the fiddler on the Roof," they must have asked, "Would it spoil some vast eternal plan, if I were a wealthy man?"

Then, as if by miracle, Jesus had come by teaching about the kingdom, preaching repentance, and calling people to follow him.

He had even extended a special call to James and John: Leave the nets and he would make them fishers of men. Could this be the beginning of the kingdom they had longed for? Had God so smiled on them that by God's grace they had been singled out to be among the closest companions of the Messiah who would restore the kingdom of Israel?

Month after month they had followed Jesus as he walked from village to village in Galilee, preaching, teaching in parables, and doing mighty deeds. Then, at last, he had announced that they were going to Jerusalem. Surely this would be the climactic moment. They could hardly wait to get there. How would he do it? By what stroke of power would he unseat the vicious Romans, rally the people, march to the temple, and declare the advent of God's kingdom?

They were so excited at the prospect of revenge, triumph, and glory that they scarcely paid attention when Jesus said to them:

> See, we are going up to Jerusalem, and the Son of Man will be handed over to the chief priests and the scribes, and they will condemn him to death; then they will hand him over to the Gentiles. (Mark 10:33)

Jesus was always talking in riddles, and they had never really figured out what he meant by the "Son of Man." All that mattered was that they were on their way to Jerusalem. Surely after all they had seen Jesus do there could be no doubt: power and glory awaited them in the holy city. The dreams that had seemed so distant were now so close to fulfillment that they could taste their sweetness.

III.

Only one thing could make it better, and that was if they could have the seats of power and honor at Jesus' side in the new age. And even though they were just a motley band on their way to Jerusalem with thousands of other pilgrims at the time, the only thing they could see standing in the way of the complete fulfillment of their dreams was that Jesus might give the seats of honor to others of the disciples. It was a small thing, but it nagged at James and John until they decided that they would just approach Jesus directly. Maybe he would even be impressed with their confidence about his ability to restore the kingdom to Israel.

They waited for just the right moment, when they could talk to Jesus alone. When the moment presented itself, they hardly knew how to broach the subject: "Teacher," they said, "we want you to do for us whatever we ask of you." As soon as they said it, they probably kicked themselves. What a clumsy thing to say! It made them look so small and conniving. But Jesus did not cut them off. There was still hope: "What is it you want me to do for you?" This was their chance. They had to go for it. They had nothing to lose and so much to gain: "Grant us to sit, one at your right hand and one at your left in your glory."

They held their breaths and watched Jesus closely. Time stood still. If their first request had been clumsy, the second was outrageously bold. But didn't they have as much right as anyone to expect such a reward? Like faithful supporters in a long presidential campaign, they had followed Jesus from one rubber chicken dinner to the next, gathering people to hear Jesus, then protecting him from the crowd. Mark tells us that Peter, James, and John were the three closest to Jesus. Now it was payoff time.

Jesus' response seemed only to be a final test of their conviction:

> Are you able to drink the cup that I drink, or be baptized with the baptism that I am baptized with?

More strange talk. Drinking the cup usually meant some act of sacrifice or suffering. But what baptism was Jesus talking about this time? Was Jesus just testing their loyalty to him? They at least had no doubts. They had left everything to follow him. But, more importantly, they could not imagine that their devotion would ever run slack.

Without giving it a second thought they both pledged their self-confidence: Certainly, "We are able." Then came the response that stunned them:

The cup that I drink you will drink; and with the baptism with which I am baptized, you will be baptized; but to sit at my right hand or at my left is not mine to grant, but it is for those for whom it has been prepared.

Jesus was telling them that they would be tested and perhaps even meet the same violent fate that lay ahead for him in Jerusalem. If all they looked forward to was a political office in the new kingdom, they would be bitterly disappointed. But that did not mean that great things did not lie ahead for James and John—only that the future would not be as they had planned it. In God's providence it would be different, and—though they could not see it—better.

Later legend has attempted to complete the story. James was in fact martyred in Jerusalem about the year AD 62, but we are less sure what happened to John. Tradition maintained that he journeyed to Ephesus and lived to be an old man there, finally repeating over and over again, "Children, love one another. It is God's command, and it is enough."[2]

But there are all sorts of stories about how he met his death. Some say that he led his followers out of Ephesus, instructed them to dig a grave, blessed them, and then lay down and expired. Tertullian reports that he was boiled in oil in Rome, but emerged unhurt. The Mandaeans said that he was starved to death in prison. Another popular legend was that he was forced to drink poison, but drinking the cup did not hurt him. The last verses of the Gospel of John indicate that some thought he would not die until the Lord returned, so during the Middle Ages there were stories of John wandering the face of the earth and meeting King Edward the Confessor of England, as he waited for the Lord's coming.[3]

Whatever became of John, this conversation with Jesus changed the course of his life. It was a second call to discipleship. When the ten heard Jesus' response, they were angry with James and John. Angry that the two had sought to out maneuver them, angry that James and John might gain some advantage in their common quest for greatness.

So, Jesus began to outline a new way for all of them. The kingdom would not be the kind of kingdom they had expected. It would be a spiritual reign, not just a political or national one. In his kingdom they would not lord it over each other the way tyrants did in earthly kingdoms. No, in this order greatness would be measured by service to others. And that service would be an end in itself, so that they would not be consumed by ambition. Their service to others would be selfless. It would not simply be a means to advantage or reward. Like the Son of Man himself, the greatest of all would be the servant of all.

Jesus was talking about a complete reorientation of life, a total conversion. Rather than grasping for oneself, energy would be channeled into doing for others. Instead of living for personal gain, Jesus held forth a vision of what life could be if each were preoccupied with what he or she could do for someone else.

IV.

This second call to discipleship must have had its effect. Another of the legends about John, and one that may have some basis in fact, is reported as a true tradition by the church Father, Clement of Alexandria, who says that after exile on Patmos, John used to go to the neighboring districts and in some places to appoint bishops.[4] At a certain place—some say Smyrna—he saw a young man of strong body, beautiful appearance, and warm heart. "I commend this man," he said to the bishop, "to you with all diligence in the face of the church, and with Christ as my witness." When the bishop promised to watch after the young man, John returned to Ephesus. The bishop took the young man into his home, brought him up, looked after him, and finally baptized him. But, when he relaxed his great care and watchfulness, some of the boy's friends corrupted him. First they led him on by expensive feasts, then they started out at night for robbery and took him with them, then they urged him to greater crimes. He gradually became accustomed to crime, and Clement says, "like an unbroken and powerful horse starting from the straight way and tearing at the bit, [he] rushed all the more to the precipice because of his natural vigor." Finally he renounced his salvation, formed a band of robbers, and became their leader, excelling in violence, murder, and cruelty.

Time went by. Then John returned and said to the bishop, "Pay me back the deposit that I left with you."

At first, the bishop was puzzled, thinking that he was being blackmailed for money that he had not received. But when John said, "I ask back the young man and the soul of the brother," the old man groaned deeply and said, "He has died."

"How and with what death?" John asked.

"He has died to God," he said, "for he turned out wicked . . . and finally [became] a brigand, and he has taken to the mountains with an armed band of men like himself."

So John rode, just as he was, straight from the church and into the mountains. As he approached the camp, he was seized by the lookout and taken to the captain. When the robber captain recognized John, he turned and fled in shame. But John followed, forgetting his age and calling out, "Why are you running away from me, child, your own father, unarmed and old? You have still hope of life. I will account to Christ for you. If it must be, I will willingly suffer your death, as the Lord suffered for us; for your life, I will give my own."

When the robber heard this, he tore off his weapons and began to tremble and weep bitterly. He embraced the old man, pleading for himself as best he could, as he was baptized a second time in his own tears and those of the aged apostle.

How often it is that our second baptism is a baptism with tears. This story, if it is based on truth, shows that John's second call to discipleship set a new course for his life. Like Jesus, he would lay down his life if necessary for a young man who had such potential and about whom he cared so much. In his second story John is a changed person—he is not looking for any personal reward beyond rescuing the young robber from the path he had chosen.

Maybe John would turn out to be one of the greatest of the disciples after all, cleansed of his self-serving ambition and distinguished by the way Christ had been able to use him in the care of others. Like Emily Dickinson, he could say,

God gave a loaf to every Bird—
But just a Crumb—to Me—
I dare not eat it—tho' I starve—
My poignant luxury. . . .

I wonder how the Rich—may feel—
An Indiaman—An Earl—
I deem that I—with but a Crumb—
Am Sovereign of them all.

V.

When we left Haber Hill Culpepper, he was seeking his disclosure of the Divine, reading poetry and philosophy. That day, however, was his birthday, so they invited the parson for tea.

The maid was in the kitchen serving when they heard a clatter, and Haber Hill went to investigate. He found the teapot shattered and the maid, who always worked barefooted, hobbling in pain with a burned foot. After he got her to sit down, he found a plastic pan and filled it with cold water. Without giving it a thought, Haber Hill knelt before her and lifted the old working woman's scarred and lined foot out of the water. Suddenly he felt

> the absolute poverty, the utter selfishness of his own life. What marks of earnest work did his pale and soft pampered body bear? Where was there so much as even an infinitesimal scratch to bear witness to a useful and purposefully lived life?[5]

Carefully and caringly he wiped her feet with a towel and returned to the sitting room. He knew that if a true epiphany, "if some profound essence of divine disclosure were forever to elude him," he had at last received his "but a crumb," and that was enough, and maybe even more than he deserved.[6]

VI.

What about it? Do you look with envy at the loaf that someone else has received while you have only a crumb? Are you still looking for a left or right hand seat in some kingdom of your own making, or have you heard Jesus' call to discipleship, perhaps even a second call to a second baptism, a washing in tears, a call to take up the towel and wash the feet of others in the place of Christ. That is the call that we extend today. It is an invitation to a total reorientation of life under the Lordship of Christ. Just imagine. . . Could it be?

Notes

[1]Sunny Rogers, "The Crumb," in *New Stories from the South: The Year's Best, 1988* (Chapel Hill: Algonquin Books of Chapel Hill, 1988) 177-90.

[2]Jerome, *Commentary on the Epistle to the Galatians*, 6.10.

[3]These and many other legends about the Apostle John are summarized and documented in R. Alan Culpepper, *John, The Son of Zebedee: The Life of a Legend* (Columbia: University of South Carolina Press, 1993).

[4]Clement of Alexandria, *Who is the Rich Man That Shall Be Saved* 41 (quoted by Eusebius *Ecclesiastical History* III. xxiii. 6-19).

[5]Rogers, "The Crumb," 188.

[6]Ibid., 190.

✝✝✝

Surviving the Test

Luke 4:1-13

Paul Duke

There are certain things that can be said with certainty about every person in this room. We know that every one of us is dying. We know that every one of us has a longing for something more. And we know that every one of us is facing temptation. No matter who we are or what we believe, no matter how weak or how strong we feel ourselves to be, we are all being tested, all under fire; we are making monumental choices.

To be human is to be tested. To be human is always to have options—options to do the better thing or the cheaper thing, options to be enlarged or diminished. To be human rightly is to be on a long journey, a pilgrimage toward maturity. But at every turn on this pilgrimage we are faced with real choices. At every juncture we choose: to regress and become less than we are, or to fixate and be stuck where we are, or to advance in the way that leads to new growth and maturity. The choices we must negotiate are constant, and the cumulative consequences of all our choices are terribly real. The New Testament word for these choices is a Greek word that means literally to go through the fire. We translate that word into English as *testing* or *temptation*.

Jesus of Nazareth was human. Like every human he had to face the fire, to make hard choices that would have real consequences as to who he became. Like the rest of us, he was free to make cheap choices. Had he done so, he would not have fulfilled his destiny. He didn't have to be the Messiah. It wasn't all fixed. He had hard choices to make. He was tempted.

Do you take any comfort in the fact that Jesus the Christ underwent fierce temptation? Here's a comfort you can take: To say he was tempted is to remember that being tempted is no sinful thing, only the human thing. To feel the pressure in your life between good and evil isn't a sin, it's a sign that you are free to choose evil or to choose good.

But there's something frightening as well in the fact that Jesus was terribly tempted. For what this means is that it's not just the lowest and weakest and meanest part of us that will be tempted. The highest and strongest and noblest in us will also be tempted, and this may be the hardest test of all. Not only does our testing never end, but the more we grow (if we grow), the more mature we become (if we ever mature), the more complicated and difficult and hugely dangerous our temptations may become. No matter how much we think we've learned about ourselves, none of us can afford to be careless or smug about our souls, none of us can assume we are safe. If we are being faithful at all, the likelihood is that the hardest test for us is yet to come.

The temptations of Jesus were a higher altitude of testing than any of us has faced. His particular tests are almost incomprehensible to those of us who still live down here in the canyons. We've never fasted forty days and pondered turning stones to bread—though our appetites are plenty tested and we are tempted to use the things of nature unnaturally for ourselves. We've never been tempted to bow to Satan in exchange for having all the kingdoms of this world—though we are tempted every day to gain some worthy end by some ungodly means. We've never been tempted to leap off the tops of temples to prove who we are and how much God loves us—though our insecurity constantly seeks false ways of assurance and cheap comfort. Let's not speak specifically, then, of his temptations—let's speak of mine and yours. What does the tempter come whispering to you? How are you tempted to regress and go backward or to fixate and be stuck where you are instead of growing in obedience, faith, and freedom? If this weren't Jesus' story but yours, if you were to write—"In my wilderness the tempter urged me to make three cheap choices"—which three would you write?

Would one of them be some Temptation of the Appetite—an inclination to satisfy yourself wrongly; to feed yourself and withhold from the hungry; to seek false comforts in what can be bought; to be sexually unfaithful; to seek empty entertainments instead of greatness of spirit; to pile up more possessions than you have any right to own? If we follow Jesus, we travel light. We learn to take less, to need less, to give more, to trust more. The devil comes and whispers lies about what we need to be satisfied and secure. Maybe one of our severest tests is the Temptation of Appetite.

And would one of your three great tests be some form of Temptation to Despair? Sinking into cynicism about the world, thinking the worst of others, wearing your heart like a fist when God has called you to kindness and to see the world with generous eyes? Or giving up on yourself in some way, ceasing to try, not reaching any more for the best that you are, sinking into personal cowardice, and settling for half a life? Or giving up in some way on God, praying too small or not praying at all any more, giving up the daily fight for faith that's honest and alive, collapsing into self-pity or pride or the functional atheism that no longer seeks the way of God? There are many forms of the great Temptation to Despair.

And perhaps one of your great temptations is the one T. S. Eliot called "the greatest treason; to do the right thing for the wrong reason."[1] This is the Temptation of Motive: "serving" in order to gain recognition and praise; "helping others" in order to get what we want from them; "praying" in order to use God for our own purposes; "sacrificing" our time and effort for all the right causes, but doing it more to salve our guilt or to serve our sense of superiority than for the sake of love. Who among us isn't tested by Temptations of Motive?

In naming the Temptations of Appetite, of Despair and of Motive, perhaps I haven't touched on the greatest tests you have been facing. You might very well give different names to your temptations. But do name them and know them. Know your own heart, including its darkest corners, its weakest positions. During these days of Lent, why not do as Christ did in the desert and face what your real temptations are? You could do worse than actually to write it down: "In my present wilderness the evil one has whispered to me, and these are my present temptations. . . ."

Now how do you survive them? Where will you find the wisdom and the courage to make choices for life and for growth instead of choices for stagnation and regression, disobedience and death? We have no simple answer or quick fix. But we have the pattern that was set for us by Jesus. We have the model of where he found his wisdom and courage. He found it in the scriptures. He had filled himself up with living words.

Three times the devil comes to him with options. Three times there rises to the mind of Jesus a word from the Word of God. Three times he finds his way to say, "It is written," and by those words he walks further on his way.

He didn't have a Bible with him. He didn't go trekking into the desert with scrolls in his arms. He faced the fire, as we all do, with whatever he had stored up inside him. And who knows how hard it may have been for him to find the word he needed under fire. Once his test began, who knows how many minutes or hours or even days of struggle may have passed before the right word distilled and came to clear focus for him as an answer. We don't know. What we do know is that he had stored such words inside himself, and in the rigors of his testing they rose to him like a hand and became his answer.

One day I was walking through the desert and the devil came and presented a fierce and complicated test to me. So I reached down deep inside myself for an answer. And what did I find in my memory? Reels and reels of old T.V. shows, some catchy tunes, and the telephone number for Pizza Hut delivery. This won't do.

Do you know how much it matters what you store inside yourself—what you gaze upon and reflect upon, what you hear, what you read and give yourself to remember? The soul sends down its roots into the soil of memory, and draws up what is there. It is crucial that we nourish the soul with what will strengthen. This doesn't necessarily mean filling up our minds with religious material. Much of what passes for Christian books and music will make you as shallow as the *National Enquirer* will. And much of what we call "secular" literature and drama and music will take you to the very gates of God. The point is that we let our souls drink deep from what will grow us toward God. The apostle Paul was pointing us this way when he said, "Whatever is true, whatever is honorable, whatever is just and pure and lovely and commendable, if there be any virtue, anything worthy of praise, think on these things."

In particular, to drink deeply from the Holy Scriptures is indispensable for us if we are to survive our testing. The Bible in your hand is food for your spirit, insight for your confusion, strength for your weakness, courage for your fear. The Bible is not a little god or a good luck charm. It's not a collection of moralisms; it's not the voice of your mother; it's not a little religious duty. It is a rope thrown down to pull ourselves up by. It is our memory. It is the calling of our true names. It speaks the living Word of the living God to the real needs of the lives we are living under fire. Read this book, read it daily and deeply. Learn these words and pray these words. Plant them like seeds in yourself and return to them again and again. Don't do it for what it pays you today or how it makes you feel today. Do it for what you will need to find within yourself on the day that will come when you are tested.

A final word. There's one thing Jesus did that you must never do. He was in his desert by himself. Don't you do it. You don't have to. Let somebody go at least part way with you. I could tell you Jesus is already there with you and that you can call on him for help, and I'd be telling the truth. But I fear you'd end up mostly talking to yourself. You need a human face to talk to. It's not for nothing that the New Testament calls the community of faith the very Body of Christ in the world. Don't keep your temptations a secret. Find yourself a sister or brother who will hear you and pray for you and help you tell the truth. I said Jesus went in alone, but that isn't quite the truth. Luke says he went in with the Holy Spirit. We find that Spirit alive between us as we help each other face the test.

I don't know how much courage you find inside yourself when you are under fire. I don't find much in me. We need partnerships to survive temptation: the partnership of scripture and of each other, and so the partnership of Christ. Turning to these, taking hold of these, we may find we are more than surviving. We may even find, in scripture's words, that "in all these things we are more than conquerors through the One who loved us." We are all in the school of temptation with Christ. Following him together, we grow in the freedom to choose the way that leads to life.

Note

[1]T. S. Eliot, *Murder in the Cathedral* (New York: Harcourt, Brace, and World, Inc., 1963) 44.

†††

Getting into the Boat

Matthew 14:22–33

David E. Garland

Our story begins with Jesus compelling his disciples to get into the boat to go before him to the other side (14:22). Commentators give all kinds of explanations about why Jesus has to compel the disciples to get into the boat. They frequently appeal to the context in the Gospel of John 6 where, after feeding the five thousand, the throng is about to come and take Jesus by force and make him king. Some say that Jesus is trying to get the disciples away from these worldly types. Others speculate that it was the disciples who were behind it all in the first place, egging on the crowds and leading the cheering section. Jesus tried to get rid of the ringleaders.

But on a purely personal level, I fully understand why you have to compel someone to get into a boat with storm clouds brewing on the horizon. Because of a checkered history in the Navy as one afflicted by acute seasickness, that is precisely what you would have to do with me—compel me to get into the boat. For whatever reason, Jesus says: "Everybody in the boat. Now!" My heart would be sinking along with my stomach. But he constrains the disciples to get into the boat to cross the lake on their own, while he abandons them to hike up some mountaintop to pray all alone.

After a night of row, row, row your boat merrily against wind, the disciples have made it all the way to the middle of the lake—right where the deep waters are. The water has always symbolized for Israel the abode of threatening powers (Ps 18:7; 32:6; 69:2). The Psalmist says that God broke the heads of the dragons in the waters (Ps 73:14), but who knew if God got all of them lurking down there? It is also the darkest hour of the night during the fourth watch, and Matthew tells us that "the boat was tormented (beaten) by the waves, for the wind was against them." When the waves are against you, a boat is not the greatest place to be in the midst of a treacherous sea.

Secundus, the silent philosopher, was said to be in dialogue with the emperor Hadrian, playing what seems like a game of twenty philosophical questions. Secundus responds to the question, "What is a boat?" with a series of word associations with which I resonate. A boat, he says, is "a sea tossed object, a foundationless home, a well crafted tomb, a wooden cubicle, a flying prison, a confined fate, a plaything of the wind, sailing death, an open cage, uncertain safety, the prospect of death." "What is a sailor?" Secundus replies, "a neighbor of death." In my opinion, here is a man who knows boats.[1]

But I would add to the list of questions, What is a church? or a union of churches? And I would answer that a church sometimes feels a whole lot like a boat: storm tossed, unstable, progress difficult and slow, being tormented by some windy opposition, with a whole lot of folk who have neither the heart nor the stomach to fight the waves. And the Lord seems to be far off hidden in the hills. When the waves start coming over the prow, and the boat starts doing the dipsy doodle in the deepest part of the sea and at the darkest hour of the night, I'm ready to be out of here. Why, Jesus, did you abandon us to this crazy cockleshell that is being swept by gale force winds and swamped by the waves? Why, Jesus, do you not come by here to rescue us from this boat and lift us up to stand on good old solid rock.

The story assures us, however, that we are not forsaken at the mercy of a howling sea; the unseen Lord sees us. The story assures us that the Living One, who is Master of winds and waves, will surely come quickly for our deliverance, even if it does take till the fourth watch of the night. So Jesus, who Matthew tells us is Emmanuel, God with us (1:23), strides across the storm-tossed sea to rescue frightened, confused disciples. Jesus, who Matthew tells us will save his people from their sins, can also save them from sea squalls.

But the passengers' vision is dimmed. Jesus is half seen, half unseen. When he makes his grand entrance, the disciples think it is phantom or some Galilean sea monster, and they cry out from fear. They don't know whether to reach for their ghost buster gear or to jump out of the boat and to take their chances with the waves—or to pray to the Lord—if they only knew where he was. One thing is clear. They are more afraid when Jesus shows up than when he is gone.

Jesus seeks to calm their fears with a word: "Take heart, I am; have no fear." Clarence Jordan translates it in corn pone English in his Cotton Patch version. "Take it easy, boys, it's just me, don't be so scared." From this translation, one gets a picture of Jesus as a good old boy chomping on a straw and wearing a soiled baseball cap with a seed company logo on it. But the one who comes to them walking on the whitecaps isn't some good old boy. It is none other than old "I AM." After all, it is only God who can tread the waves. It is Emmanuel who comes to them.

Job tells us that God alone tramples the waves of the sea (9:8). It is only God who has walked in the recesses of the deep (38:16). Both the Psalmist and Isaiah tell us that God makes his way through the sea, through the mighty waters (Ps 77:19; Isa 43:16). And that must go for God's son too, because here he comes strolling across the depths of the abyss. He does not come to them on a calm, sunny day; his striding across the heaving sea at the peak of its strength is a token of his conquest over the powers of chaos.

And Peter is willing to chance that it just might be the fellow they left on the shore, so he bellows out, "Lord, if it is you, command me to come to you on the waters." "Lord, if it is really you, get me out of this leaky tub." "Make me walk on water too." I know exactly how he feels. e.e. cummings wrote: "King Christ, this world is all aleak, and life preservers there are none."[2] If you have ever been on a perilous boat that is bobbing as a cork and that is beginning to look like the Lusitania, the Titanic, and the Dorian Grey all rolled up into one, you want to get out of there. Like Peter you want to yell out, "Lord, if you are anywhere out there, get me out of here!" Jesus obliges Peter and says, "Come." Peter takes a few steps, takes a look at the wind, and then takes a fall. He becomes terrified. The translations say that he begins to sink, but the word that is used appears in 18:6 where it means "to drown." Peter is spitting water, and that should hardly surprise anybody. If you try to walk on water, you will sink like a rock—unless you are God.

But Peter is still able to gurgle out, "Lord, save me!" Notice the change. None of this, "Lord *if it is you,* save me" business, but "Lord, save me!" I guess when you are about to go under for the third time your vision clears, and you know now that the Lord is indeed out there. Peter has enough wits about him to sputter a cry for help, and Jesus has enough grace about him to stretch out his hand and to catch him immediately. Only then does he berate him as a "little faith." That is a nice thing about Jesus; he saves before scolding. Most of us might have been tempted to let Peter flail about and go under a couple more times. The lesson might get through to him better.

Perhaps I am being too hard on Peter. Commentators usually commend him for venturing out onto the seas. They say things like, "Peter steps out on faith." "Peter does not go until Jesus gives the word, and Jesus helps us do the impossible." "If Peter only had kept his eyes on Jesus, instead of the waves." But I beg to differ. Getting out of the boat and trying to walk on water is not faith in my book; it is foolhardiness. It is not what Jesus called disciples to do. Nevertheless, the commentators assure us that Peter is the representative disciple and the church is to learn a lesson from this. But what is the lesson? What is the church supposed to do?

Jesus rebukes Peter for his doubt, "Why did you object?" The question is, when did he begin to doubt? Readers may too quickly assume that Peter doubted when he became frightened by the gale-force wind; but the text does not say that he doubted, rather, that "he became afraid" (14:30). He first expressed his doubt when he asked the question, "Lord, if it is you. . . ." He therefore left the boat in a context of hesitation about whether it was really Jesus. Doubt had already crept into his heart when he demands, "Lord, if it is really you, prove it! Make me able to walk on water too!"

There are three other places in Matthew where people put "if" questions like this to Jesus. When Satan tempts Jesus, he goads him, "If you are the son of God, tell these stones to become bread" (4:3). "If you are the son of God, cast yourself down and let the angels catch you" (4:6). When the high priest interrogates Jesus, he commands him, "Tell us if you are the son of God or not" (26:63).

When the passerby jeer Jesus on the cross, they taunt, "If you are the son of God, come down from the cross" (27:40). Is Peter's demand any different? "If it is you Lord, make me walk on water." It is no less wrong than these other challenges.

The first thing wrong with it is that the demand is induced by doubt. The second thing wrong with Peter's desire to walk on water is that it is due to the same impulsive bravado that will lead him to even greater failure later in the story when he denies his Lord three times (26:35). The third thing wrong with it is that disciples have no business trying to walk on water. That is the old sin of pride, wanting to be like God, rearing its ugly head again. Jesus did not call disciples to be sensations; he called them to be his servants. Notice that when they get back into the boat, Jesus does not say to the disciples, "Now, did everyone see what Peter did wrong here. Let us all try this again until we can get it right." And then you have a parade of disciples walking on water and scaring the bejabbers out of other poor, unsuspecting fishermen.

The problem is that Peter audaciously wants to do what Jesus does: to skip on the waves, to become master of all things, to be omnipotent and omnicompetent—all for God's glory, of course. A lot of disciples would like to be great for Jesus' sake. A lot of disciples want to be lifted up above the lesser mortals around them, although they may clothe that base desire with religious dress— then they can do great things for God's kingdom. We all face the temptation to want to be above it all and above everybody else, and Peter audaciously wants to do what Jesus does. But the difference is this: Jesus is coming to save the boat, and Peter wants to make a spectacular exit. If he can walk on water, he won't need the boat any more. He can leave those other dullards in the boat behind.

In Matthew's story, however, one cannot abandon the boat. The story places the emphasis on the boat. It is the *boat*, not the rowers, that is tormented by the waves. The end stress suggests that the most important thing happens when Jesus and a dripping-wet Peter get back in the boat. It is when they enter the *boat*, that the wind ceased. It is then that those in the *boat* worshiped him, Jesus, saying "Truly you are the son of God!" What is important happens in the boat!

One of the lessons of this story then is to stay in the boat. This is a hard word for someone who may not like boats. I know what it is like to feel confined in a leaky tub in a dogma-eat-dogma world. I know the temptation to want to be above it all—to want to step out of the boat and say, "Eat in my wake." I know the temptation to say to others, "I don't need you; just look at what I and Jesus can do on our own without you." But the boat is where we belong—with all the others. And, frankly, it beats trying to walk on water, because we know what will happen if we try it. We will start to drown in the overpowering sea. As disciples we are better off in the boat. I think Grady Nutt was right when he compared the church to the ark. If it weren't for the storm outside, you couldn't stand the stench inside.[3]

And if you are a disciple, you signed up to get into the boat to help row, to help hoist the mainsails, and to bail out the bilge water in a long and perilous journey to the other side. Our job is to confess Jesus as the son of God, not to walk on water. Leave that to God and the son of God. Jesus is not revealed to the world through our amazing ability to leap tall buildings at a single bound, to be faster than a speeding bullet, or to walk on water. We don't have to walk on water, if we can just baptize a few with water. We don't have to be faster than a speeding bullet, just smarter than a speeding bullet—and not loose cannons taking pot shots at everybody else in the boat. We don't have to leap tall buildings in a single bound, if we can just take little leaps of faith—like getting into the boat in the first place, like committing ourselves to discipleship and following Jesus.

Perhaps Jesus does help us do the impossible. He helps us to stay in the boat even when we are tossed about with many a conflict and many a doubt and when there are a whole lot of fightings within and fears without. If we stay in the boat through the storms, however, Jesus will not fail to save us and help bring us safely to the other side.

Note

[1]David Aune, ed. *Greco-Roman Literature and the New Testament: Selected Forms and Genres*, SBL Sources for Biblical Study 21 (Alanta: Scholars Press, 1988) 120.
[2]e. e. cummings, *Collected Poems* (Publisher unknown, 1938) 258.
[3]From the great and good oral tradition of the sayings of Grady Nutt.

†††

Take Up the Towel. . . .
Take Up the Cross!

John 13:1-20

W. Hulitt Gloer

They had gathered for what would be their last supper. For three years they had been together, marching up and down the hills and valleys of Galilee and Judea. During those three years they had seen and heard incredible things, but nothing more incredible than what they were about to see. Jesus rose from the table and walked toward the door. He took a towel and wrapped it around his waist. He poured water from a pitcher into a basin and one by one he washed the disciple's feet!

Footwashing . . . it had to be done. After a day, indeed, after an hour on the dusty trails of Judea, it had to be done. So a basin and a towel were standard equipment in every Judean home. But footwashing was a do-it-yourself affair, considered so demeaning, so degrading that a Jewish slave could not be required to wash his master's feet. Yet here was the master washing his disciple's feet.

Two-thousand years later it is hard for us to imagine just how shocked those disciples must have been. We have domesticated this story by constant rehearsal. Still we may catch something of their surprise in Peter's question as Jesus approached, "Lord, do you wash my feet?" For Peter and for all the others, it just didn't make sense. Footwashing was no job for Jesus.

Remember with me the context in which this event occurred. For three years they had traveled through Galilee and Samaria and Judea with Jesus. They had seen him demonstrate incredible power —power over disease, power over the demonic, power over death itself. In fact, they had just come from Bethany where Jesus had raised Lazarus from the dead. Now they had arrived in Jerusalem to the accolades of the cheering throngs who welcomed Jesus as

the messianic king; the king come at last to reestablish the throne
of David. The disciples must have been riding high as they
gathered in that upper room. The latest public opinion polls indi-
cated that Jesus' approval rating had never been higher. Buoyed
by this latest wave of popular support, the disciples were ready to
get on with the revolution . . . and then this . . . the pitcher, the
basin and the towel. It just didn't make sense. "Lord," Peter asks,
"do you wash my feet?"

Considering the circumstances Peter's response is not at all
surprising. There in the upper room that night Jesus was defining
messiahship in ways that ran counter to everything that Peter and
the others had been taught to believe. In fact, there in the upper
room with a towel in his hand Jesus was fleshing out a vision of
God that flies in the face of all human expectation. Here was a
God of power and might taking the form of a servant. Here was
a picture of God that was as incomprehensible as it was incredible.
"Lord," Peter exclaimed, "you will never wash my feet!" In his
mind it just didn't make sense. Footwashing was no job for Jesus.

Do you remember Jesus' response? "Peter," he said, "if I do not
wash your feet, you have no part with me." It was a way of
saying, "Peter, this is who I am, the Son of Man who came not to
be served but to serve. This is who I am Peter, and unless you are
willing to accept me for who I am, you have no part with me."
The fact is, of course, that Jesus had been trying to prepare his
disciples for this ever since they began their journey to Jerusalem.
On at least three occasions he had set his messianic destiny before
his disciples and at the same time their destiny if they would be
his disciples.

At Caesarea Philippi Jesus had confronted the disciples with
the question of his identity (Mark 8:29). He asked them, "Who do
you say that I am?" Peter responded with a bold confession, "You
are the Christ," and upon hearing this confession Jesus began to
teach his disciples "that the Son of Man must suffer many things
and be rejected by the elders and the chief priests and the scribes,
and be killed . . ." (Mark 8:31). And upon hearing that Peter took
Jesus aside and began to rebuke him! Imagine it if you can, Peter
rebuking Jesus! Why? Because in Peter's mind messiahs don't
suffer and die. In Peter's mind messiahs march into Jerusalem in

power and glory, messiahs drive the godless Romans into the sea, messiahs set up the throne of David and reign over all the king-doms of this world. All this talk about suffering and death just didn't make sense to Peter, and with his response to Peter, Jesus makes the reason clear. "You are not thinking the things of God but of humankind" (Mark 8:33). In other words, Peter, you have an agenda and God has an agenda but they are not the same agen-da. Immediately, then, Jesus summoned the multitude with his disciples and said, "If anyone wishes to come after me, let him deny himself and take up his cross and follow me" (Mark 8:34). The sequence makes the message clear. Jesus was announcing his destiny and, at the same time, the destiny of all who would be his disciples. "This is who I am Peter, one who came to offer himself for others in suffering and death, one who is bound for the cross and all who would be my disciples must be willing to take up that cross too."

As they continued their journey to Jerusalem, Jesus again spoke of his destiny. "The Son of man is to be delivered into the hands of men, and they will kill him . . ." (Mark 9:31). When they came to Capernaum Jesus asked his disciples what they had been discussing on the way, but they kept silent because they had been discussing who among them was the greatest (Mark 9:34). While Jesus looked ahead to a cross, the disciples were measuring for their crowns. While Jesus spoke of suffering and death, the dis-ciples were debating position and power. He had spoken clearly of his own destiny and then in the face of their blindness, he spoke of theirs. "If anyone wants to be first, he shall be last of all, and servant of all" (Mark 9:35). The way of suffering service was Jesus' way, and it must be their way too.

When they had almost reached Jerusalem, Jesus spoke of his destiny once again. "Behold we are going up to Jerusalem, and the Son of Man will be delivered to the chief priests and the scribes; and they will condemn him to death, and will deliver Him to the Gentiles. And they will mock Him and spit upon Him, and scourge Him, and kill Him . . ." (Mark 10:33-34). With these words Jesus had set his destiny before his disciples for the third time. He had come among them as one who would suffer and die. And the disciples response? Believing that it was only a matter of time now before Jesus would establish his kingdom in Jerusalem, James and John came campaigning for the most prestigious and powerful positions in the king's cabinet. They wanted to sit at the king's right and left hand. They wanted to be the secretary of state and the secretary of defense (Mark 10:35-37). While Jesus was announcing cross-purposes, they were caught up in career planning! So he called the disciples together to speak of their destiny if they would be *his* disciples.

> You know that those who are recognized as rulers of the Gentiles lord it over them; and their great men exercise authority over them. But it is not so among you, but whoever wishes to become great among you shall be your servant; and whoever wishes to be first among you shall be slave of all. For even the Son of Man did not come to be served, but to serve, and to give his life a ransom for many. (Mark 10:42-45)

Jesus came to serve and to give his life for others, and those who would be his disciples must be willing to serve and give their lives too.

Now do you see what has happened? Three times Jesus announced his destiny, defining it in terms of suffering service. Three times the disciples listened to what Jesus said . . . listened, but did not hear. And we cannot help but wonder why. Perhaps they did not hear because they could not hear. They had the scenario all worked out for Jesus. He would march on Jerusalem, drive the Romans into the sea and establish the throne of David once again. And when it happened, they would be there at his right and left hands. Yes. . . . They had it all worked out and the plan did not include a cross. So blinded by their preconceptions, they simply could not hear.

Or perhaps they did not hear because they would not hear. Satisfied and secure with their own agenda, they weren't really interested in his. Unwilling to abandon their visions of kingdom power and glory, they could make no room for suffering and service. So they listened to Jesus, . . . but they did not hear. Still on the way to Jerusalem he had told them and there in the upper room that night, taking up the towel, he showed them. And they watched in awestruck amazement as one by one he washed their feet.

Taking up the towel was but prelude to and preparation for an even more shocking event, for less than twenty-four hours later this same Jesus would hang suspended between heaven and earth on two crossed wooden beams, nails in his wrists and feet and a crown of thorns on his brow, arms outstretched as if to take the whole world in his embrace, with little more than a towel to protect him from the elements. Having taken up the towel, he would take up the cross, giving himself away in love, painting the ultimate portrait of God on the canvass of human history. "This is who I am, Peter, and unless you can accept me for who I am, you have no part with me."

But there is something else that we must see. On all three occasions when Jesus had spoken to his disciples about his destiny, he also spoke to them about theirs. And did you notice that in each case the sequence was the same? First Jesus announced his own destiny. Then the disciples demonstrated that though they had listened to Jesus, they had not heard. Then immediately Jesus spoke about the destiny of those who would be his disciples. The implication is clear: It is only as we understand who Jesus is that we are able to understand who we must be if we would be his disciples. He stands before us as the one who came not to be served but to serve and to give his life a ransom for the many. He calls us to take up the towel, to take up the cross, to follow him as servants of the world.

That was his call to them on the way to Jerusalem, and then to make sure they understood that night in the upper room he took up the towel to wash their feet. And when he had finished, this is what he said:

> Do you know what I have done to you? You call me teacher and Lord; and you are right, for so I am. If I then, the Lord and the teacher, washed your feet, you also ought to wash one another's feet. For I gave you an example that you also should do as I did to you. Truly, truly, I say to you, a slave is not greater than his master; neither is one who is sent greater than the one who sent him. If you know these things, you are blessed if you do them. (John 13:12-17)

"I have given you an example," Jesus said, "that you should do as I have done to you." On the road to Jerusalem he told them. In the upper room he showed them. To be a follower of Jesus is to be the servant of the world. It is to take up the towel. It is to take up the cross. "This is who I am, Peter, and this is who you must be!" Oh, there are other ways to go, ways that are more attractive, more reasonable, more comfortable. Indeed, there are as many counterfeit crosses as there are hands to fashion them. But the cross that Jesus bore is the service of the world, and whether we hear him or not, it is to take up that cross that he calls us.

Every ten years the citizens of the little village of Oberammergau, Germany reenact the story of Jesus' death in their world famous Passion Play. Thousands of people travel from all over the world to witness this drama. For many years the part of Christ was played by a man named Anton Lang. It is said that on one occasion Lang was being interviewed by a group of reporters. One of these reporters had watched as for hours day after day Lang had carried the huge, heavy wooden cross. He suggested to Lang that there might be ways to lighten the heavy load that he bore as he carried that cross. Why not have a cross fashioned out of plastic or balsa wood or fiberglass. It would still look like the cross and no one would ever know the difference. Lang's response to the reporter's suggestion is telling. This is what he said, "If I cannot feel the weight of the cross, I cannot play the part."[1] The weight of the cross is the service of the world. Nothing else will do. Are you prepared to take it? "I have given you an example, that you should do as I have done." Take up the towel. . . . Take up the cross!

Note

[1]Though this story has reverberated in my mind for years, I have never been successful in locating its original source.

†††

Will the Real Minister Please Stand Up?

Numbers 11:1-30; Mark 9:38-41

John H. Hewett

Moses had a problem. He'd led the Children of Israel into the wilderness on the hunch that any God powerful enough to turn the mighty Nile into blood and slay the first-born sons of Egypt could handle the logistics of food, water, and shelter for this wandering multitude. And, in truth, God had provided. Water had gushed from the rock at Rephidim. And manna had appeared every morning for two years. For two years the Israelites had gathered it, ground it, boiled it, and kneaded it into something resembling dirty bread. They'd had three square meals of manna every day for 730 days: fried manna, roasted manna, manna casserole, mannaburgers—they were sick of manna! (And you think you get tired of turkey by the Sunday after Thanksgiving!)

After two years of this, an insurrection broke out in the camp, led by the rabbis, who had a strong craving for fish, and fresh fruit, and lambchops seasoned with onions and garlic. They called themselves the Back to Egypt Party. Their platform consisted of one word: meat. They were tired of living with dry mouths. They were as hungry for something fatty and juicy as a patient discharged from a Seventh Day Adventist hospital! They had a strong craving for cholesterol. They moaned, and groaned, and wept, and bitterly complained to Moses, who had gotten them into this culinary hell. They were a little too loud with their griping, however, and God heard them. God got angry and came looking for Moses. Moses was holed up in his tent with some warmed-over manna hash, singing his favorite country song, "Why me, Lord?"

Why have you done this to me? Why do you hate me so much, that you've given me one million whiny Israelites to wet-nurse? Did I conceive all these people? Am I their mama, that you can say to me, "Carry them, feed them, and burp them all the way to Canaan? Where in the world am I going to find a butcher in this wilderness? They come whining to me: 'Give us meat! We want meat! We demand meat!' "

Listen, O Yahweh of the burning bush, O summoner of frogs and flies, who made me say, 'Let my people go'. . . . This is too much for me. They are too many for me. If this is the way it's going to be from now on, kill me right now. Put me out of their misery, and out of mine.

The Lord had pity on poor Moses. "Find seventy of the elders you can trust, and bring them with you to the tent. You're right. This is too much for one person. I'm going to shift all this burden from one to seventy-one. And tell the people they'll have meat tomorrow, and every day for the next month. They're going to eat meat until it runs out of their ears and they weep for a salad. The Lord has heard. The Lord has spoken."

Moses summoned the seventy as God had commanded, and the Lord put the spirit on them all. When the spirit fell, the whole group began to tell the good news of God. And then a funny thing happened. Eldad and Medad were running late that morning, and were still in the camp when the spirit fell. So they started preaching right there where everybody could see and could hear. That was too much for Joshua, Moses' executive officer. He ran to find Moses and tell him that two elders were back in camp preaching, speaking for God. That was Moses' job. Nobody else was supposed to speak to God or for God but Moses. Moses was the only prophet God had authorized. At least, until that very moment.

Moses—tired, weary, suicidal Moses—says to Joshua: "Your jealousy for my sake is touching, old friend. But I wish the spirit had fallen on all Israel, and not just seventy. I wish every man, woman, and child clamoring for meat, starving for the food of slavery, would hunger and thirst for righteousness this morning, would crave the good news of God's redemption. Would that we were all prophets, filled with the spirit and satisfied with the food of God!"

Did Moses know what he was saying? Probably not. But what you see in Moses is the anxiety overload that comes to every person who has been set apart to speak for God. Sooner or later, you start to wish all those people could listen to God for themselves.

II

If we are honest, we see forms of that "ministry burnout" in Jesus. He weeps over Jerusalem, wishing he could mother them, but it cannot be. He sends out his disciples two by two to do the same work he's been doing, but laments when they seem to miss the point. He's constantly being chased around Judaea and The Galilee by thrill-seekers demanding signs and wonders, or a little more fish and bread. Now when he works a miracle, he cautions, "Don't tell anybody. Just keep it to yourself."

When Mark reports that a traveling prophet is healing people in Jesus' name without being ordained, Jesus rebukes, not the free-lance minister, but the Twelve.

> Don't try to stop him. If he's doing mighty works in my name, then he's part of the solution, not the problem. If he's not against us, he's on our side. Even the lady who gives you a cup of water because you're following me is doing mighty acts for the King-dom, and God notices it all.

Jesus knew he couldn't make it to every village, heal every blind man and bleeding woman, raise every comatose child to life. He didn't call the Twelve just to set forth a symbol. He needed the help! "Follow me, and you'll fish for people," he said, knowing that you're more likely to bring in a worthy catch when you have more than one line in the water.

The Twelve occasionally figured this out. In that they were more successful than the Children of Israel, who were out gather-ing food when the spirit fell, and missed it. The Lord sent quail to the camp, meat two yards deep a day's journey in every direction.

And the Twelve Tribes, who had learned to trust God for daily bread and manna tomorrow, went crazy. They spent all day and all night and all the next day gathering the quail into bushel baskets, preparing for a feast. But before they could swallow the first bite, the hand of the Lord struck against their watering mouths with a deathly plague. They would come to call that place Kibroth-hattavah—the graves of greed.

III

There are two lessons here. Be sure you get them. They're as crucial to the future of this church and the whole Christian movement as they were to the Israelites, who paid scant attention, and the Twelve, who kept on asking a question Jesus had already answered.

The first lesson is this: the Spirit, which blows and lists where it will, has endowed all of us with special gifts for ministry. This is not surprising. There is work to be done, and God needs our help.

When I fracture my leg, I can pray for healing and call in the elders of the church to anoint me with oil. I should also call an orthopedist who has invested four years of college, four years of medical school, and four to seven years of residency in response to God's call to be a healer. God cooperates for good with doctors and nurses in the work of healing: they do what only they can do, and God does what only God can do. In the process, broken people are mended.

Your gifts may be different. Some of you teach, others work with your hands. Some exhort, some administer, some serve, some manage, some count, some nurture, each according to the gifts distributed by the spirit.

All gifts given to Christians are for the service of God. God uses what you and I do to build up the Body of Christ, to equip the church for the work of ministry, to bind up the wounded and mend the broken. All of us are ministers here. I do not list my occupation as minister, but as pastor. I get paid to be a pastor. I am a minister by the grace of God. And so are you.

We have a problem, though. We pay certain people to serve the church, and we call that full-time vocation "the ministry." We used to read the King James Version of Ephesians 4:11 as textual support for hired clergy to do the church's work:

> And He gave some, apostles; and some, prophets; and some, evangelists; and some, pastors and teachers; for the perfecting of the saints, for the work of the ministry, for the edifying of the body of Christ.

My, what a comma can do! It can lead to the development of a false ecclesiology. For centuries only priests were allowed to read the Scriptures. Only priests could administer the sacraments. Only priests could baptize, and only the bishop could ordain.

Though we Baptists arose out of the ferment of the Reformation, we remain imprisoned by that comma. Though we, the people, have the power to ordain, we set others apart to do the work of ministry. They distribute the bread and cup to the rest of us. They go into the waters of baptism with our children. They marry and bury. They preach the Word. We send them to win the lost. And, if we are not careful, they become the hired hands whom we pay and expect to do the church's work.

We offer them a false respect, you know. We put our "ministers" up on a pedestal, forbidding others to breathe that heady air. Their prayers are more spiritual, their visits more personal, their prophecy more vital. And, like Joshua, we get a little anxious when we see other people out doing the prophet's job.

The first lesson is this: take that comma away! Moses thanked Joshua for his protective concern, but wished aloud that the spirit had fallen on all God's people. Jesus told the Twelve to widen the boundaries of their authority to include every person who acted for God in the name of Jesus. What Paul wrote to the Ephesians was this:

> To each one of us grace was given according to the measure of Christ's gift. He gave some as apostles, and some as prophets, and some as evangelists, and some as pastors and teacher, for the

equipping of the saints for the work of ministry, to the building up of the body of Christ.

If we need a new title for clergy, Paul suggests one: "coach." Better yet, "player coach." The task of those whom the church has set apart is to equip the rest to do the task God has assigned everybody. On this team, there are no first or second strings, no red-shirted players taking a year to get ready, no one on waivers. The only list that will keep you out of the game is that of the injured reserve; we do tend to our wounded.

It's important enough to our ecclesiology that we print it on our worship order every week:

> Believing in the priesthood of all believers, First Baptist Church ministers through the gifts and abilities of all its members. The congregation has called particular persons to the special tasks of equipping and enabling members to share the gospel of Christ with the whole human family.

Who are the ministers at First Baptist Church? You're looking at them. There's a balcony full of them. Here's a choir with nothing but ministers of music robed and ready. Down here are row after row of grace-gifted Christians gathering for practice, learning new plays, gaining strength, getting ready once more to enter the contest.

"Would that all the Lord's people were prophets, and that the Lord would put His Spirit on them!" Moses WAS a prophet. In Jesus Christ, that is precisely what God has done.

IV

There is a second lesson: get it, too. The Spirit falls in all manner of places, some seemly, some not. There is too much to do, and too little time, for us to waste the daylight rebuking those who don't do God's work our way. This morning in Asheville fellow-believers are reading the King James Version and the Reader's Digest Bible. They're singing baroque anthems and Stamps-Baxter gospel songs, shaped-note hymns and charismatic choruses. Some are whooping and hollering, some murmur "Amen," and some are fast asleep. Some are wearing Brooks Brothers suits and some are wearing their work clothes. Some aren't even in church: they're going cell to cell at the jail, or missing worship in order to drink coffee at Shoney's with a hurting friend. Some are proclaiming the end of the world, and some preach as though they've got all the time in the world.

Listen: we're not in competition with them. If they're telling the good news of Jesus Christ, they're not against us, they're on our side. And we're on theirs. If the spirit falls on them before they make it to the tent, let them prophesy in the camp. For one day, my brothers and sisters, we're all going to make it to the kingdom, and you'll be surprised at how much whooping and hollering God will allow from his joyful children—the kingdom, where "Amen" is never whispered but always shouted from the rooftops.

Therefore, Paul wrote, since we have this ministry, we do not become discouraged, for we do not preach ourselves but Christ Jesus as Lord, and ourselves as your servants for Jesus' sake.

Now, hear the living Christ calling you to a life of full-time Christian service wherever you go. Feel the power of the Spirit poured out upon all God's people, even you.

What you are, brother, what you are, sister, is a minister!

So live as one:

> —as though Christ himself has called you;
> —as though the whole church depended on you;
> —as though you have enough power to change the world;

For He has. . . .
And it does. . . .
And you do.
Amen.

†††

The Unshakable Kingdom

Hebrews 12:28

D. Leslie Hollon

"Therefore, since we are receiving a kingdom that cannot be shaken, let us be thankful, and so worship God acceptably with wonder and awe." (Hebrews 12:28)

What happened in that moment struck me as I pulled into my own garage one afternoon. What soul pulsation sent a friend and fellow disciple to death? Deciding to kill himself and not his engine, he closed the garage door. The collected poisonous fumes fulfilled his wish to be taken out of this world's gloom of two failed marriages and two children beyond his reach to parent.

Days before his saintly mother had gone to check out her fears about her son's depression. Knowing worship's power she guided him to a church famed for its worship. But on this fateful Sunday, an unusual focus directed the worship experience and the hoped-for renewal did not arrive. They exited emptier than they had entered.

I don't know whether a different worship style from that church would have rekindled hope within her son and saved his life. But I do know that until her own death, she believed that a great Sunday experience—that answered his questions by once again showing him God's unshakable Kingdom—would have birthed a rediscovered hope into her despairing son. Such is the hunger for God's kingdom power and what worship can do.

We are Kingdom seekers. We search for a Kingdom where we are known and loved. We search for a Kingdom possessing the treasures of our happiness. Whether in places, people or purpose we search for a Kingdom that will grant us full citizenship. And in this citizenship—with all the privileges and responsibilities thereof —we hope to fill our soul pockets with everlasting joy.

Having placed this desire within us, God knows this search of ours. And so walking from heaven to earth came Jesus, preaching Kingdom. The one, true Kingdom where our purpose, place, and people flow us into the Promised Land.

Knowing that only God's Kingdom remains after all others have been shaken—Jesus refused to sell out his divine mission for lesser realms. Jesus came as the Kingdom King to show us the way. Fulfilling the meaning of his own prayer for disciples— "Worshiped be God, and Thy will be done on earth as it is in heaven"—Christ cleared the Kingdom highway on which all Kingdom searchers are to travel. Those who actually do the traveling are called disciples. Disciples of "the King of Kings and Lord of Lords."

Kingdom disciples, like the author of Hebrews, understand that Kingdom privileges bring Kingdom responsibilities. So with discipleship's clarion call this writer encouraged persecuted Christians to "fix their eyes upon Jesus, the pioneer and perfector of our faith, who for the joy set before him endured the cross, scorning its shame, and sat down at the right hand of God's throne."

A Disciples' Learning

The word disciple carries its meaning—learner. Christian disciples are learners of Christ. Putting this learning into practice is a lifelong Kingdom journey, for along the way are many wanting our full allegiance. Promising to provide us with a place to stand, a people to stand with, and a purpose to stand for, these pretenders to the throne will mislead us into thinking that it is *their* kingdom that cannot be shaken.

If we lose sight of Jesus, our kingdom desires will lead us into temptation and have us worship for the approval of human kingdoms. Again and again this sin has struck me deaf and dumb.

Half my life ago I went to Miami as a youth delegate to a national political convention. There I met many of the world's most potent political leaders. I shook the hand of the reigning American president whom I had just helped to re-nominate to represent my party and our country.

As a faithful disciple of this kingdom movement I returned to my college campus with a message that this man, his vice-president, and their message were trustworthy: that allegations of their involvement in the Watergate burglary and similar crimes were false.

I was the last one to see the light that exposed them "as parading Emperors with no clothes." I didn't see the light because *I didn't want* to see the light. I wanted them to be that which they weren't—messengers building a lasting kingdom on earth.

But I alone was at fault for my sin. For my lusting earthly heart wanted to worship a person and a kingdom I could help control. Not until months after the Convention, and the subsequent election, in which I had joined with others in so successfully selling the lie that our king took the throne by a landslide—did I see the light. There on national television was the person I had served and whose hand was no longer shaking mine but holding the pen that resigned him from office.

On that night, my idol fallen, I saw Christ more clearly. Kings of this world are mortal and only by "fixing my eyes on Jesus" will I know how to be in this world but not of the world. Only by "fixing my eyes on Jesus" will I know how to be of heavenly good in our world for which Christ died.

Discipleship isn't a Christian's escape route from life's challenges but the empowerment by God to greet these challenges with a character ready for the task. Through the holy experience of encountering God we are shown the way to Kingdom success.

Worship, "fixing our eyes on Jesus," is the key to discipleship success. By using biblical standards to shape our definition of success, we find Kingdom happiness. *Success* is being who God made us to be and doing what God called us to do. *Faith* is the strategy. *Hope* is the vision. *Love* is the power. As the author of Hebrews knew, the heart's comprehension of biblical success comes only by worshiping God with awe and wonder.

For in worship—whether in private or public—we *still* our hearts to know God. Knowing in the biblical way is personal relationship. Knowing God as our Creator, our Redeemer, and our Comforter is *awerobics*. Knowing that God's desire is to give us treasures—love, joy, peace, patience, kindness, goodness, faithfulness, gentleness, and self-control.

A Disciple's Waiting and Acting

A successful knowing flows from the worship rhythm of waiting and acting. *Waiting* on God's vision to show the way. *Acting* on the vision received from our waiting. To *act* when we should *wait* forfeits the promise. To *wait* when we should *act* forfeits success.

The worship rhythm of praise, confession, gratitude, and submission can be as obvious to disciples as seasons of the year are to farmers. In each season farmers know what to do and with each worship dimension disciples also know the direction we are to pursue. *Wanting* to know is essential.

The morning after a closing session of the Missouri Baptist Convention, I was standing in the hotel's check-out line with Calvin Miller. The day's sun hadn't yet risen and I was sharing my gratitude for his stirring sermon given the night before. Then I asked him what he most hoped for from his recently announced move, in which he was leaving a successful long-term pastorate to be a seminary professor. His answer? "To know God better!" Although a nationally respected author, teacher, and pastor, he realized there was more to know from God. He knew that his key to success was in direct proportion to his knowledge of God.

Dietrich Bonhöffer, a powerful World War II Christian martyr, wrote in *Creation and Fall* that Adam's and Eve's *first* sin was not eating the forbidden fruit. Instead, it was talking *about* God rather than *to* God. There in creation's most beautiful sanctuary—the Garden of Eden—the father and mother of all humanity made the fundamental mistake of not seeking God's counsel.[1]

Thinking they knew all there was to know from God, Adam and Eve failed miserably when confronted with the temptation to find success by eating from the tree of forbidden knowledge. Their fallen pride shut them off from worshiping God at the very moment when worship was what they needed most. What a price they paid to discover that the key to success is the waiting and acting rhythm of worship.

When they needed to be silent before God, they spoke. When they needed to wait upon God, they acted. When they needed to trust the truth of God, they let themselves be misled by fallen pride.

Sound familiar? It does for all of us who are "like sheep gone astray, turning each unto his or her own way." But the most amazing thing happened to Adam and Eve. What God did to them after their sin was even more incredible than making the stars, the oceans, the land, and the animals. The Lord God, Creator of all the universe, forgave the sinners. Adam and Eve were then able to walk into the future—East of Eden—because they were forgiven.

Forgiveness brings hope, and hope is a disciple's cornerstone. So, because of God, Adam and Eve felt confident and gave birth to Cain and Abel. As parents, they taught them worship's importance. Abel learned from his parents' mistake and worshiped God without arrogance, but Cain, filled with fallen pride, worshiped himself—causing his work to become his kingdom.

Success for Cain was what he could produce by "the sweat of his brow." Master of his own fate he could tease God by pretentious worship acts. Success for Abel, however, came from knowing God and that all of life was a God-given gift. By knowing God, Abel could know himself and from this knowledge, Abel's spirit worshiped. He understood that without God there isn't spiritual life and *without* spiritual life there isn't success and *absent* success there isn't happiness and *minus* happiness there isn't joy for living.

Consequently, Cain killed Abel. Without true worship Cain's life was agony, and except for anger he had no reason to live. Like his parents before him, filled with conceit, he blamed others for his failed spiritual life. Cain had to accept responsibility for his failure and from this confession he was free to live again.

The story of pride building false kingdoms is the story of all people. Even for those who have never heard the name—Adam, Eve, Cain, and Abel. Deep within the recesses of each human soul is the spirit of our being made in God's likeness, and this presence of God prompts us to worship, and worship molds disciples. For where our treasures are, there dwell our hearts.

The stakes are high, eternally high. If we worship ourselves or our work or our idols, then the chain effect of hell-on-earth is unleashed—NO true worship, to NO spiritual life, to NO lasting success, to NO shalom happiness, to NO joy for living. Chaos is let loose. Only by the holy experiences of knowing God—true worship —are we set free to live.

Worship's Bigness

What happens in worship is bigger than any one of us. The size of the happenings fit God. God's presence breaks through for worshipers when we don't play games. Posturing our bodies in traditional worship positions, while our inner thoughts worship human-made gods, keeps us from reaching our God given potential in the true Kingdom.

Worship requires change and change makes us uncomfortable. When presented with God's bigness and the accompanying responsibilities, we get tempted to shrivel God to our own size, and flee ourselves from the Kingdom's call.

Through a combination of bold and subtle efforts, the resistance to let God be God comes by our attempts of limiting God to our own set of experiences, our own way of reasoning and feeling, our own realm of ambitions, and approximates our wanting to make God over in our own image. Making God into a god. An idol we can control.

Christian disciples stand in the earthly place of God's Kingdom while knowing that only in heaven can perfect bliss be found. As one friend who has ministered for forty-five years says, "Walk with your head in heaven and your feet on earth."

We are to live in the tension of the "already" and the "not yet." Through worshiping God we learn how not to get *enslaved* by mortgage payments, food consumption, sexuality, book learning, spectator sports, materialism or racism. We are to be converted and discipled by following what God promises.

The Christ *in us* shines through in proportion to our allowing the *likeness* to shape our character. And our character is the consummation of our decisions and experiences. Since what we do with our heads, hands and hearts shapes us and reveals us, we are not to conform to idols of this world but be transformed by

Christ's renewing our minds. Disciples are, as Luther said, "little Christ-ians."

As people redeemed in Christ, disciples stand in an unshakable Kingdom that is present and future, earthly and heavenly. We are as Jesus was, between baptism and crucifixion-resurrection. Living at the in-between puts us on life's cutting edge and keeps us from being dulled by the forms of this world. Paul warned "that the god of this world blinds unbelieving minds and keeps them from seeing the light of the gospel of the glory of Christ, who is the likeness of God."

William Wordsworth, the great Romantic poet, explained the dulling process as "The world is too much with us, late and soon. Getting and spending we lay waste our powers."[2]

Or as the twentieth-century Englishman Stephen Spender wrote, "What I had not foreseen, was the gradual day, weakening the will, leaking the brightness away."[3] As we worship God, allowing the indwelling presence to empower us, we walk the pathway that leads to and from heaven.

Claiming Your Kingdom

Disciples of a Kingdom that cannot be shaken follow the principle of first things first—trusting God's way for our happiness. The early church, knowing that who or what we worship determines the content of our character, framed the basic worship confession of discipleship—"Jesus Christ is Lord."

Our worship is determined by what we think will bring us happiness and who it is that we call Lord. As Jesus said, "where your treasure is, there is your heart also." The heart, biblically understood, deposits and directs our desires. Therefore, the key to successfully worshiping the one true God comes by our treasuring God.

This means disciples traveling God's way as *the* road to real happiness. The shalom kind of happiness. Where our treasure in God's presence and our heart's delight come together. The treasury of God being opened in our very midst.

When God is worshiped, we are lifted from ordinary life and taken into the realm of wonder where only faith, hope, and love have bargaining power. There and then, within the worshiper's soul, the necessary changes take place for disciples to get relief from this world's woes. There and then our energy is renewed for journeying in God's Kingdom.

Worship's hope is there for us all. Our Kingdom hunger for people, place, and purpose is satisfied by experiencing God. A Kingdom where Power is given for disciples to climb life's mountains and walk life's valleys. May we have soul "ears to hear" for around us, and maybe within us, there is life despairing— wondering whether or not to kill the car engine. Wondering whether God's unshakable Kingdom can calm a frightened soul.

Notes

[1]Dietrich Bonhöffer, *Creation and Fall: A Theological Interpretation of Genesis 1-3* (London: SCM, 1959).

[2]William Wordsworth, "The World Is Too Much With Us," *William Wordsworth: The Poems*, vol. 1, ed. John Hayden (New Haven: Yale University Press, 1977) 568.

[3]Stephen Spender, "What I Expected," *Collected Poems 1928–1985* (London/ Boston: Faber and Faber, 1985) 24.

†††

Drop Everything!

Mark 1:16-20

David M. Hughes

When Joani and I were visiting London last fall, something happened that I will never forget for the rest of my life. This incident did not take place at the Tower of London or Buckingham Palace or Westminster Abbey. No, this unforgettable event took place in a subway station, or in what Londoners call "The Tube."

It was late in the evening, and Joani and I were dead tired. We had taken a day trip away from London, and after a full day of sightseeing, we were ready to get back to the Wake Forest House and crash.

As we waited in the Tube station, we noticed that the normally punctual trains were running late. So did the hundreds of other tired passengers whose patience began to wear thin. Then a voice came over a loudspeaker, and informed us that the trains were delayed because of a security alert at another station. People groaned a bit but kept talking. Thanks to numerous bombings and rumors of bombings generated by the Irish Republican Army, folks were accustomed to being inconvenienced by this alarm and that alert.

At least three times, the voice on the loud speaker calmly told us to be patient for the delayed trains that would soon arrive. Then without warning, the same voice spoke with controlled urgency, informing us that now the police thought our very station contained a bomb, and we were to exit the station, *immediately!*

Suddenly, folks who had been half asleep jerked awake and sprang to their feet. Londoners know that bombs can maim or kill, and they waste no time responding to such orders to evacuate. But I am here to tell you that no one reacted more quickly and decisively to this command to evacuate than an American, a woman from Winston-Salem named Joani Hughes! As soon as the announcement ended, I stood and turned to say, "Let's go," to Joani, only to find that she was long gone.

Most folks were walking briskly toward the exits and up the escalators. Not Joani! I've never seen her move so fast in our eighteen and a half years of marriage! You think O. J. Simpson runs fast through airports to get his rented car? Well honey, you haven't seen anything till you've seen Joani Ray Hughes running through a Tube station away from a bomb scare! When I finally caught up with Joani outside the station and asked her why she abandoned her beloved husband, she said that she wanted to make sure her three children still had a mother alive—but she was certainly hoping I would make it! I've always said Joani was a fast woman. But that night in a London Tube station when she dropped everything and flew the coop, she proved it!

(By the way, the bomb announcement was a false alarm. A bomb did explode that night, but somewhere else. But we still have a good story to tell our children, grandchildren, and you!)

Sometimes when we least expect it, life throws us a curve ball, and at a moment's notice, we have to drop everything and go. That sort of response doesn't particularly suit those of us who are a bit more methodical about life. We'd rather take a "wait and see" approach, and eventually react in our own good time. But sometimes life doesn't give us the luxury of strolling about casually. Sometimes, all we can do is drop everything and run.

If you don't believe it, just ask Peter, Andrew, James and John. For brothers Peter and Andrew, it had all the appearances of being just another day on the Sea of Galilee. As they had done a thousand times before, these suntanned fishermen cast their nets into the water, and in due course began to draw up nets bulging with fish. Nothing could be heard except the quiet lapping of the water against their boats.

Suddenly, a piercing voice rang out from the shore. "Follow me," the voice said "and I will make you fishers of men." None of the fishermen on the sea that day knew exactly who this man was, but there was no mistaking the authority in that voice. Then, to the amazement of nearby fishermen, Peter and Andrew dropped a net full of fish, and bolted for the beach. Before folks could recover, they watched James and John drop the nets they were mending, and follow this same man without so much as a word to their flabbergasted father, Zebedee.

Now, Jesus had the first four of his twelve disciples. And the bystanding fisherman had a strong suspicion that their normally rational, responsible fishing buddies had flipped their lids and walked off the deep end.

We have heard the story of Jesus' call of the disciples so many times that it's easy to overlook what a positively stunning scenario is described here. Most of us for one reason or another have been tempted to walk off the job, or out of the family at a moment's notice because we've had it up to here and we can't take it anymore. But most of us don't act on those feelings, because mature, responsible adults don't just walk off the job or out of the family. And yet, that's precisely what Peter, Andrew, James, and John did.

Jesus said, "Guys, drop everything, and follow me." And incredibly, these four and eight others did. And in so doing, they give us clues about what we must drop to answer Jesus' call to discipleship today.

For example, we learn that to be disciples of Jesus Christ we must drop our blinders and see the light.

Thanks to all the hoopla surrounding the inauguration of President Clinton this past week, our minds have been on the American presidency more than usual. One of the more fascinating books about a president is one written by Robert Caro about another Southern, democratic president named Lyndon Baines Johnson. Some of us remember LBJ for his famous War on Poverty. Others of us may remember him for his infamous conduct of the Vietnam War. Younger members of our congregation may simply remember him as the man who became president when John Fitzgerald Kennedy was assassinated. Caro found, however, that the people in the Hill country of Texas where Johnson first began his career as a congressman remember him for something else.

Caro notes that when he was interviewing in the Hill Country, no matter what he was talking to people about, one phrase was repeated over and over again concerning Johnson. The phrase was, "He brought the lights. No matter what Lyndon was like, we loved him because he brought the lights." They were talking about the fact that when Johnson became congressman from the Hill

Country in 1937, at the age of twenty-eight, there was no electricity there. And by 1948, when he was elected to the Senate, most of the district had electricity.[1]

"He brought the lights." That's precisely the claim Matthew, quoting Isaiah 9, makes about Jesus Christ. Only, Jesus did not just bring electrical light to the Hill Country of Texas. He brought eternal light, the light of the Kingdom of God to the whole world. "The people who sat in darkness have seen a great light, and for those who sat in the region and shadow of death light has dawned."

There is one catch, however. In order to see the Light, we must remove whatever blinders we may have on. Remember there were plenty of folks in Jesus' day who observed Jesus at close range—hearing him teach and preach, seeing him perform miracles—but they never saw the Light. Why? Because they refused to remove blinders like Pharisaism or legalism or loyalty to Rome or loyalty to self. For these and a hundred other reasons, they refused to see the Light, refused to repent of their sins, and consequently, refused to enter the Kingdom of heaven breaking out all about them.

The same holds true today. Today, the blinders may be different—money, power, secularism, hedonism, atheism—but the results are the same. Folks refuse to see the one who brought the light to the whole world. And sadly, where discipleship is concerned, they don't even get to first base.

But seeing the Light, important as it is, doesn't tell the whole story. In fact, there are folks who apparently see the Light, only to hide it under a bushel. And that sort of inaction just won't do, because this passage tells us that to be a disciple of Jesus means dropping our delay, and going for broke.

You are probably familiar with that time-honored story about the board meeting Satan called in Hell. Having assembled his cabinet, Satan says to his senior advisors: "We need to develop a strategy for wreaking havoc upon the earth. Do you have any suggestions about new ways for reaching human beings for our side?"

One advisor suggests, "Tell them there is no heaven."

Another says, "Tell them there is no hell."

But the prize winning suggestion is judged to be far more effective: "Tell them there is no hurry."

Judging by the blase nature of much of the church today, you would have to admit that this diabolical scheme has worked brilliantly. If our favorite basketball team was down twenty points with ten minutes to go in the game, we would be dumbfounded if our team slowed the game down and sat on the ball for the rest of the game. And yet where our commitment to Christ and his kingdom is concerned, many of us play as though we've got all day, with no hurry or urgency or intensity whatsoever.

Jesus never has, and never will approve of such a lacksadaisical approach. In many respects, one word stands out above all others in our passage for today, and that is the word "immediately." "Jesus said to them, `Follow me and I will make you fishers of men.' *Immediately*, they left their nets and followed him."

I challenge anyone within the sound of my voice to show me one instance in the New Testament where Jesus called folks to discipleship, and then said, "Relax, friends. There's no hurry on this deal. You go home, think it over, and then have your people call my people when you're ready to give me an answer." That line simply ain't in the Book.

Of course, being a disciple of Jesus doesn't always mean walking off your job or out of your family. But it does mean realizing that you don't have all day, and neither does the world. Every minute you sit around on your can, vacillating, equivocating, or just falling asleep in the pew, the world goes to hell on roller skates. If you think you've got all day, my friend, to get it together for Jesus, you better think again.

Recently, William Willimon, chaplain of Duke University, shared a personal story in the *Christian Century*. He writes:

> When I was serving a little church in rural Georgia, one of my member's relatives died, and my wife and I went to the funeral as a show of support for the family. It was held in a small, hot, crowded, independent Baptist country church. They wheeled the coffin in and the preacher began to preach. He shouted, fumed, flailed his arms.
>
> "It's too late for Joe," he screamed. "He might have wanted to do this or that in life, but it's too late for him now. He's dead.

It's all over for him. He might have wanted to straighten his life out, but he can't now. It's over."

"What a comfort this must be to the family," Willimon thought sarcastically.

"But it ain't too late for you!" the preacher continued. "So why wait? Now is the day for decision. Now is the time to make your life count for something. Give your life to Jesus!"

It was the worst thing I had ever heard. "Can you imagine a preacher doing that kind of thing to a grieving family?" I asked my wife on the way home. "I've never heard anything so manipulative, cheap, and inappropriate. I would never preach a sermon like that."

She agreed with me that it was tacky, manipulative, and callous.

"Of course," she added, "the worst part of all is that it's true."[2]

Make no mistake about it, friends. Being a disciple for Jesus means dropping our delay, and *immediately* going for broke for the kingdom. But that's not all. It also means dropping *our* fishing nets, and following *the* Fisherman from Galilee.

The late T. B. Maston made a statement in a Southwestern Seminary class years ago that a student named John Mills wrote down in his notebook. Maston told the class, "All the claims of Christ can be summed up in two words—'Follow Me'." When John wrote that significant statement in his notebook, he placed a question mark in the margin. He wondered whether that was an overstatement.

Recently, after a career in ministry, while John was preparing for his move to a new home in retirement, he came across that notebook and reread the statement. He erased the question mark from the margin, and then wrote, "I am convinced that the only way to win the world is to understand Jesus' challenge and take seriously all that it implies."[3]

What does it mean to be a disciple? You can sum it up in two words: "Follow Jesus." And what does it mean to follow Jesus? It means to drop our nets, rearrange our priorities, and reorder our lives about Christ. It means to go as Jesus went, serve as Jesus served, do as Jesus did. Matthew tell us that Jesus went about teaching and preaching the gospel, and healing folks of disease. If you want to be a disciple, then you, too, in your own God-called way will be sharing and serving, helping and healing, feeding and forgiving. If you want to be a disciple, you'll "follow the footsteps of Jesus, where'er they go."

A pastor tells of making a hospital visit. The hospital seemed unusually quiet as he made his way down the hall to visit a church member who had suffered a stroke. After knocking on the door, he entered the room and before he spoke, the daughter said, "Daddy, guess who has come to see you?" He immediately replied, "It's my preacher." The daughter, surprised at his accuracy, asked, "How did you know that?" The father simply replied, "I know that walk."[4]

Later, when he reflected on this comment, the pastor realized that his member had recognized the sound of his footstep. But then he wondered how many who heard and saw him walk would know that he walked as Jesus walked.

Not a bad question, is it? Friends, how many people recognize simply from the way you walk that you are a disciple of Jesus? If you are not sure, then I have one word of advice—"Drop everything! And start walking, *immediately*, for Him!"

Notes

[1]The anecdote and quote are taken from *Extraordinary Lives*, ed. William Zinser (Boston: Holden-Mifflin, 1988) 197-231.

[2]William Willimon, "Take Heed to Yourselves," *Christian Century,* 3 December 1986, 1085-86.

[3]This story is taken from a sermon by Rick Lance entitled "Following in His Steps," *Preaching* (July/August 1989): 18.

†††

Alternatives to Anxiety

Matthew 6:25-34

Peter Rhea Jones

Worry can rip away the quality of your life. Fritz Perls believes that anxiety is the stopping block of life.[1] Some worry routinely because of temperament or the example of a parent. Some wrestle with insecurity because they have been roughed up by a recession. Some feel pangs of anxiety living alone without a spouse. Nearly all of us know the distressing anxiety that assails us in the night and robs us of sleep.

I have known anxious feelings about life and ministry, and as a boy of seven faced the prospect of early death. Such frantic feelings can paralyze. And you can become anxious at mid-life because you have not become what you ought to be or could have been. You too can be anxious lest you cease to be. If tossed aside by a restructuring, a devoted disciple would be looking at unemployment and worried about food for the table and clothes for growing children. Your own sense of worth is frayed, and God can seem as distant as a decade.

The disciples of Jesus were not devoid of common human feelings of anxiety when they were on mission as disciples. They were itinerant missioners who gave up their jobs to follow Jesus and to proclaim the gospel of the kingdom. Paul Scherer used to speak of their abandoned life with an adventurous God. The original disciples were those like Jesus who lived without a trade and in the care of God. And naturally they became concerned about what they would eat the next day and expressed their worry to Jesus. They could come on board a boat, discover only one loaf of bread, and anxiously say: "We have no bread" (Mark 8:16). They were facing the special circumstances of living an insecure existence without a regular income.[2] And the Son of Man himself had no place to lay his head (Luke 9:58). He too had left carpentry shop and family.

A faith missionary feels the anguish of depleting funds and an end of provisions for the mission itself. A Christian in a corporate culture who quietly insists on personal integrity stands exposed to the possible loss of security. A minister taking a prophetic stand or accepting an unsettled church risks loss of job and even calling. A terminated minister "between churches" experiences storms of anxiety about tomorrow. A person called into ministry uproots a family from the relative security of friends and finances and journeys to seminary without enough money to purchase provisions for two months. There is built-in insecurity for the disciple on mission. On mission the disciple leaves himself and herself vulnerable, and sometimes unforeseen and uncontrolled life circumstances thrash the sense of well being of a Christian.

With his distinctive authority Jesus confronted his own disciples, "I say to you, Do not continue to be anxious about your life" (Matt 6:25). With the use of the imperative he forbids the continuation of their anxious worry. The anxiety prohibited involves "any undue concern or crippling anxiety (an attitude) that drives one to seek security by one's own efforts apart from the Father (an activity)."[3] Anxiety about the future must not master our lives. While it is basic in human life to desire to secure life in this world,[4] the prisoner of worry lacks an inward freedom. Thus Jesus outlaws excessive concern and offers an alternative, "a summons to faith".

The conquering of anxiety is an essential element in our text,[5] and the celebrated "Song of Freedom from Care" offers the disciple effective alternatives to crippling worry.

First, FOCUS ON THE PRESENT (v. 34). Taking the end of the passage first, listen to one effective way to handle worry. Center on the present as a strong alternative to fear of the future: "Therefore, do not be excessively anxious about the next day, for tomorrow will be anxious for itself. Let the hardship of the day be sufficient for itself."[6]

Here is not only wisdom for life but a coping skill for the disciple in the midst of mission. Center responsibly in the now and do not borrow trouble from the future.

We often worry about things that never happen. "I am an old man now"—the words were carved by a monk on the wall of his cell—"I am an old man now: I have had lots of trouble; and most of it never happened."[7] Worry comes from anxious anticipation, a fear of the future. Someone said that worry is interest paid on trouble before it comes due. And Robert Orben believed that it does not pay to worry because if you went through last year's file marked "Important," chances are the only things you'd keep are the paper clips. Perhaps we should abandon our anxieties since they do not really achieve anything.

Our passage opens up the possibility for living abundantly in the present rather than being ravaged by fearful thoughts of the future. The disciple can learn the art of living a day at a time in daily dependence on God. A boy in high school tried not to be anxious, but he stayed worried about the three G's: grades, girls, greenbacks (or, as the girls would say: grades, guys, and greenbacks). One day his Sunday School teacher met him at his place of employment and noticed a glum look. "Why are you so glum? Why do you look so sad?" And the youth replied, "Well, I am kind of down today." With a down to earth savvy his Sunday School teacher countered: "Why don't you try the old numbers method?" The high school student skeptically thought to himself, "What in the world is the old numbers method?" The teacher explained; "Well, the old numbers method means simply taking one thing at a time." So the high school student tried it and found it a helpful beginning.

Jesus, the master psychologist and physician of the soul, encourages you as a contemporary disciple to focus on the present. He knew so well that anxiety draws our attention away from the present and diminishes the immediate.

John Wesley, preaching on our passage, urged Christians to live for today. "The future is nothing to you," he declared, because "it is not yours; perhaps it never will be." And one theologian criticized the tendency of some college students to understand the present moment only as a preparation for the future, getting ready for later responsibilities. Instead, live in the present coping and growing. The Christian leader Bonhöffer, commenting on verse 34, left the legacy of these words for serious disciples; "live every day as if it were your last."[8]

In the popular song "One Day at a Time," a woman addressing "Sweet Jesus" asks for strength to do every day what she had to do. Since yesterday's gone and tomorrow could never be hers, she prays, "Lord, help me today, show me the way, one day at a time."

One genuine alternative to paralyzing anxiety lies in the home-spun secret of one day at a time. Since the present has to do with mission for the disciple, limiting scope allows for manageable parameters and frees the Christian for the primary task.

Second, PRAY. Another powerful alternative to anxiety lies in prayer. It contains antidote to anxiety, even a vehicle for venting your worries and concerns to Someone who loves and understands completely. Instead of being tied up in anxious knots let your requests be made known to God. In the process of praying you find liberation from anxiety.

Yet Jesus seemingly says nothing of the therapy of prayer in the "Song" (Matt 6:25-34), so is it really appropriate to drag petition in as an alternative to anxiety? The answer seems a ringing "yes." Our text as a whole offers a correlative to the fourth petition of the Lord's Prayer: "Give us this day our bread for the coming day." Our text may well be an expansion or interpretation of this part of the "Our Father."[9] Now clothing for warmth and food for sustenance represent primary human needs, but the alternative to anxious care for the disciple lies in praying and specifically evoking the Disciples' Prayer. And we pray for our provisions (6:11). The solution is prayer spoken in trusting confidence in the provisions of the heavenly Father. Our needs are not eclipsed by our devotion to the kingdom. Yet in our devotion to the Kingdom they are put in perspective.

Other powerful prayers elsewhere in the New Testament relate petitionary prayer to anxious feelings. These prayer texts invite the disciple to turn anxious concerns over to God. We find in 1 Peter encouragement to cast our anxious feelings on God because he cares for us (5:7). We do well to turn in our Bibles and underline in red the sentiments in Philippians that we can turn to in anxious moments: "Have no anxiety about anything but in everything by prayer and supplication with thanksgiving, let your requests be made known to God" (4:6, RSV). And then claim the promise of the following verse: "And the peace of God, which passes all understanding, will keep your hearts and your minds in Christ Jesus" (RSV). We need not waste our emotional energies on fearfulness when we can take our anxieties to God.

F. W. Boreham told the moving story about a person who took his cares to God. During the early days of his ministry Down Under he went to call on one of his older church members. Entering the room where the elderly man lay, he noticed a chair pulled up next to the man's bed. "I see that I am not your first visitor today," said the pastor. The old man then began to explain the presence of the empty chair.

It seems that when he was a small boy he had difficulty praying. His minister suggested that he overcome his difficulty by placing an empty chair in front of him when he prayed, pretending that Jesus was sitting in that chair like an attentive friend. The old man shared with his minister that he had just kept up the practice after he grew up.

The pastor left the room a short while later. After a few days the old man's daughter came to tell the pastor that the old Christian was dead. "I was out of the room only for a short time," his daughter recounted. "When I returned, he was gone. There was no change in him except I noticed that his hand was on the chair."[10] Yes, a great alternative to a debilitating anxiety is prayer, especially that which trusts in God.

Third, SET A FIRM PRIORITY. We are shoved around when we lack a firm center. As Christian disciples on mission we can yet become consumed with self-concern, mastered by tormenting obsessions with material things. Anxious pursuit of material needs can preoccupy our efforts and minimize our contribution. The secret to the defeat of anxiety lies in obedience to the will of God. As we establish the lordship of Christ as our first concern, anxiety about our life withers.

When Jesus invited his original disciples to "seek first the kingdom of God", then he offered a dynamic, positive counterpart to his early negative warnings about obsessive concern for food and clothing. "Rather above all else," the Greek suggests. Jesus portrayed a sharp contrast between anxious seeking of one's security and seeking of the kingdom. Robert Guelich points to "one's life controlling efforts," taking the word *"seek"* to mean the giving of oneself "unreservedly to the pursuit of the kingdom."[11] And Edward Schillebeeckx goes so far as to say that this pivotal verse "might be regarded as the central theme of the whole of the New Testament."[12] With the initial call to be a disciple Peter and Andrew left all and followed. They made a total break with their past. They left families and work, distancing themselves from independent income (Mark 8:34ff). Participating in the uncertain life of the traveling preacher, equipped only with bare essentials, disciples were to remain dependent on the good will of people (Mark 6:8ff; Matt 10:9ff).[13]

As the disciple settles the priority question then horizons can be widened to a focus upon the kingdom of God. Then our engaging concern is not so much how I secure my own life, but how do I serve God best. The issue is no longer security but service. We gradually or quickly grasp the Great Realization that we do not draw our life from the present world. As Christians we no longer belong to this world. We belong to the World to Come. We really are "resident aliens."

Set a priority that puts everything else in its proper place. Settle on your priority for life. Will to do one thing. And do it as a young person. Put the mission first. Announce the kingdom by all means. Tell the good news. Be salt and light. A kingdom priority is a powerful alternative to anxiety.

One other creative alternative emerges from these celebrated but highly unconventional directives to disciples. Fourth, TRUST IN THE PROVIDENCE OF GOD. A. M. Hunter reminds us of one of the charms of the gospels: that they never allow us to forget that we are living in a world where the grass grows green, the lilies bloom, and the birds sing. The gospels abound with the sights and sounds of nature. "When Christ walked the field he drew, from the flowers and birds and dew," said Hunter, "Parables of God."[14] God spreads before us the lovely sacrament of nature. Consider the wild lilies and the wild birds. Ponder well the gospel they preach. Let your prayer be along these lines:

O Lord our God, teach us to know
How beautifully lilies grow.
Give us that faith in Thy good care
Which lilies breathe in open air.[15]

The thrust of our text is indeed directed to a "looking at God, the Creator, as Provider and Sustainer rather than to one's self."[16]

Using inclusive illustrations drawn from the experience of women (toiling, spinning) as well as men (sowing, harvesting), Jesus invites his disciples on mission to "consider." Mary Magdalene points out that the word "consider" gives the feeling of restful reflection, not a peremptory glance but a long, feasting look. In considering the lilies the disciple was taught about "living provisionally"—as those for whom provision has been made.[17] As we slow down and ponder the carefree existence of an humble meadow flower, we understand the provisioning of God. The wild lily, usually identified as white, can be taken to refer to all the wild flowers of Palestine, but Dalman preferred the purple anemones because their high thistles provided good fodder for fires.[18] "I tell you," said Jesus, "not even Solomon, in all his gorgeous splendor, was ever dressed up like a single one of these" (v. 29, Williams). How much more will God clothe disciples. We are invited to a confident trust in the heavenly Father who supplies the needs of his creation.

So the disciple can be freed from a life churned up with worry to get on with mission. Believe in providence. Trust in God. Keith Miller attended a conference at Laity Lodge led by Elton Trueblood. Between sessions Miller told Dr. Trueblood in an off hand manner that he would really like to study with him. Trueblood pulled out his daily planner and told him that school started on June 7 and said, "You *were* serious weren't you?" Keith Miller had no idea of quitting work and had no money. He mumbled something about praying about it. Within ten minutes a president of a company walked up and said he was tired of putting money into buildings and would like to support conferences. He went on to say that if Miller wanted to go into this kind of work he would like to help financially.[19] So a lay person turned on to the challenges of living the Christian life found the freedom to go on mission.

One of my favorite stories about the power of providence comes from the life of J. C. Penney. During the stock market crash of 1929, he found his dry goods business quite secure, but he had made other unwise commitments that troubled him greatly. Broken physically and mentally, he was hospitalized. Overwhelmed with a fear of death he wrote farewell letters to his wife and son, not expecting to live through the night. The very next morning he awakened to singing emanating from the hospital chapel. He slipped into the chapel as the people sang, "Be not dismay'd, whate'er betide, God will take care of you." He went on to pray, "Lord of myself, I can do nothing. Will you take care of me?" He felt a weight lifted. Now he was a different person. That day he took on God as his Senior Partner.[20]

These stories of Miller and Penney do not promise instant magic for all of us, but when you look back on your own life you may notice some things difficult to explain apart from the providence of God.

In the "Song" Jesus offers you the disciple viable alternatives to immobilizing anxiety. They are worth remembering: focus on the present, pray, set a priority, and trust in the providence of God.

Notes

[1]Cited by Bruce Larson, *The Whole Christian* (Waco: Word, 1978) 90.

[2]The special context is recognized by Ulrich Luz, *Matthew 1-7*, trans. W. Linss (Minneapolis: Augsburg, 1989) 407-408. Luz scores the vital point that vv. 31-33 make clear that Jesus is not concerned with humanity in general, but the specific people seized by the kingdom. He thinks with Theissen of itinerant radicals. Obviously then our contemporary application must make hermeneutical transpositions.

[3]So Robert Guelich, *The Sermon on the Mount* (Waco: Word, 1982) 336. There is scholarly debate whether the text points to an anxious attitude of mind or frantic striving after. Both elements are actually in the context. Note the use of the word "seek" (6:27, 31, 33). Wayne Oates, *Anxiety in Christian Experience* (Philadelphia: Westminster, 1955) 9, defines generic anxiety as "a reaction of

tension to threats to the selfhood of an individual or to the groups to which he belongs. . . ."

[4]R. Bultmann, *"merimnaō," Theological Dictionary of the New Testament,* ed. Gerhard Kittel, ed. and trans. Geoffrey Bromiley, 10 vol. (Grand Rapids: Eerdmans, 1967) 4:591.

[5]Luz, 404. He supported his contention by the motif of little faith (v. 30), the formation of the questions in v. 31, and the Lukan *meteorizomai* (12:29).

[6]Guelich, 349, takes the position that the faith in God's provision expressed in the Fourth Petition of the Lord's Prayer changes the pessimistic and fatalistic tone of the evil of the present day. *Kakia* can also be translated "hardship" as well as "evil."

[7]*The Three Half-Moons* (New York: Abingdon, 1929) 185.

[8]Wesley, Schleiermacher, and Bonhöffer quoted by Luz, 409n.

[9]See Guelich, 336, following a tested theory of Bornkamm. He argues cogently that "all things" of 6:33 are food, drink, and clothing. Here incidentally is an instance of advanced critical analysis contributing to proclamation.

[10]The original source of this story is unknown.

[11]Guelich, 343-44.

[12]*Christ,* trans. J. Bowden (New York: Crossroad, 1981) 541.

[13]See Hans Weder, "Disciple," *Anchor Bible Dictionary,* ed. David Noel Freedman, 6 vols. (New York: Doubleday, 1992) 2:208.

[14]*Preaching the New Testament* (Grand Rapids: Eerdmans, 1963) 52-53.

[15]Quoted by Hunter, 56.

[16]Guelich, 336. The anxious concerns of the missioner, in another aspect, are addressed in Luke 12:11ff.

[17]*Jesus, Man of Prayer* (Downers Grove IL: InterVarsity, 1987) 23.

[18]Cited by Luz, 405n.

[19]James Newby, *Elton Trueblood: Believer, Teacher, and Friend* (New York: Harper, 1990) 183.

[20]See Charles and Ruby Treadway, *Fifty Character Stories* (Nashville: Broadman, 1969) 157.

†††

Peter the Disciple

1 Peter 5:1-4

Michael Martin

Mickey was pastor of a church in Detroit. Periodically he preached in a downtown mission that ministered primarily to street people. One such sermon was rudely disrupted by the late and noisy arrival of a drunken, filthy man who collapsed onto a back pew. It was a cold, wet Detroit evening, and it soon became obvious that the man was more interested in a warm place to sleep than he was in things spiritual. Almost immediately his snores were competing with the sermon.

When the service ended and the people departed, the drunk on the back pew still slept. As Mickey worked to wake him, he noted that the fellow was even more foul and ragged than he had appeared when he made his entrance. He did not even have shoes, but pieces of cardboard tied about his feet with string. Mickey knelt, removed his own shoes, and placed them on the drunk. His simple gracious gift to a most undeserving recipient has become a part of my personal understanding of discipleship.

Acts such as Mickey's remind me that discipleship is not primarily a concept we struggle to define, but a life we struggle to live. It is in observing the lives of faithful followers of Jesus that I have encountered the most eloquent "definitions" of modern-day discipleship. Likewise, it is the lives (as much as the words) of biblical characters that teach the meaning of following Jesus. One such character is Simon Peter.

Simon's credentials as an exemplary disciple are impressive. A successful, bilingual, Galilean businessman before he met Jesus, he was one of twelve promising young men chosen by Jesus for personal training. He was educated for three years by God incarnate. (Now some of you may have encountered educators who thought they were God incarnate, but Peter had the real thing.)

As the training of the disciples progressed, Peter was recognized as one of the best of the group, and became part of an inner circle of three disciples who attended Jesus on very special occasions in his ministry. Ultimately he was recognized as the leader of the twelve and spokesman for the entire group. Acts pictures him as a powerful evangelist, a miracle worker after the very fashion of Jesus himself, and head of the young Jerusalem church. He was highly respected in Christian communities throughout the Empire and was involved in ministry in Jerusalem, Antioch, Corinth, and Rome. He became a noted Christian spokesman and a widely read author.

Yet can we really cite Peter as an exemplary Christian disciple? After all, this is a man whom the *Interpreter's Dictionary of the Bible* describes as "volatile and impulsive and liable to failure."[1] Should we emulate someone who sank when given the chance to walk the water with Jesus and who's response to the transfiguration was to suggest a building program? (Sounds like a Baptist, doesn't he?) Should someone who denied Jesus when confronted by a serving girl serve as a model disciple?

This same Peter had to be reprimanded by Paul for demeaning Gentile believers in Antioch. His action even endangered the Gentile mission and threatened to pollute the essence of the gospel itself! The Gospels record Peter arguing with Jesus more often then any other single character. It almost seems that when Jesus gave him the designation "Petros" (rock), it was a reference to his hard head, not his solid faith.

The litany of Peter's blunders and failures seems to imply that whatever success he enjoyed as a disciple should be attributed to good intentions, dumb luck, and forgiving friends. (Don't we all wish that such was the formula for success.) Personally, I find the description of Peter as impulsive and failure-prone unconvincing. It seems inconsistent with someone who began with good credentials, was affirmed repeatedly by Jesus himself, and led in many notable ministries. Peter was not bumbling, impulsive, and liable to failure. Rather, he was an over-confident traditionalist in the process of being transformed by following Jesus.

Self-confidence is a valuable character trait. But Peter was so sure of himself that it threatened his ability to learn from Jesus. A disciple who is too sure of himself makes a poor learner. If you would learn from Jesus, you must first admit that you have something to learn. Humility is necessary, or discipleship is impossible. Peter learned humility.

In Luke 5:1-11, Jesus borrows Peter's boat and then determines to repay him with a large catch of fish. "Put out into the deep water and let down your nets for a catch," Jesus said. Peter was reluctant. Jesus, a carpenter-become-teacher, was treading on Peter's area of expertise. What professional fisherman likes to be told by an amateur where or when to fish? Reluctantly he complied, and the cocky fisherman was amazed by the results.

In Matthew 14:22-33, the disciples are terrified at the sight of Jesus walking toward their boat across storm-tossed water. Only one disciple dared asked if he might join Jesus. Peter, the disciple who sank, was not so much impulsive or fool-hearty, as he was confident, both in Jesus and in his own abilities as a disciple. His I-can-do-that-too spirit expressed a self-confidence that bordered on arrogance.

In Matthew 26:31-35, Jesus predicts that all his disciples will desert him. "I will never desert you," Peter responded. He was adamant—he would die before he would deny Jesus. He was sure that he knew the degree of his commitment and the strength of his resolve. Later that night he found out how wrong he was. At his denial he would not have had so far to fall, would not have felt so low afterward, had he not had an exalted opinion of himself beforehand.

At the beginning, in the middle, and at the very end of the Gospels' story of Peter, we find him not living as one accustomed to failure, but acting as one accustomed to success. He was confident in his own ability and convinced he was capable of being the best of the disciples. Failure came to Peter partially as the result of overconfidence bordering on arrogance.

Humility is a hard lesson to learn. But the Jesus who washed the disciples feet made it clear that the disciple who refused to learn humility could not be a disciple at all. Without genuine humility a disciple will not listen well enough to learn the truths that Jesus brings. It should come as no surprise then that a disciple struggling to bring self-confidence and humility into balance will sometimes have trouble hearing Jesus' message. Such was also Peter's challenge.

Peter, the self-confident, was so sure he knew the ways of God that he had trouble hearing Jesus. Popular religious traditions held by the disciples were repeatedly challenged by Jesus. Peter the confident traditionalist was forced to chose between masters. When they were in conflict, should he follow the tradition or should he follow the Christ? A disciple must be clear about whom he serves.

In Matthew 16:13-20, the great confession is recorded. Peter's confession is followed by Jesus' prediction of his passion. Peter rejected the idea of Jesus' death. Privately, he rebuked him: "This must never happen to you" (v. 22).

I suppose one could understand Peter's words simply as the shocked response of a concerned friend. But several things in the passage indicate that more was involved. (1) Jesus' reprimand of Peter in 16:23, "Get behind me, Satan," is the same as his final rejection of Satan's temptations to be less than God's messiah in 4:10 (*hypage satanā*). (2) The confession is followed by the transfiguration (17:1-8), during which the command issued to Peter, James and John by God regarding Jesus is, "Listen to him!" What had they not been willing to hear? Peter, at least, did not want to listen to Jesus' teachings about the messiah as suffering servant. He wanted a traditional messiah, one who rules, not one who suffers. (3) Descending off the mount of transfiguration Jesus resumed teaching about the suffering of the messiah and his forerunner (Elijah). Peter in these passages is not slow-witted, he is a traditionalist. Disciples who are traditionalists must learn to let the Lord judge their traditions rather than let their traditions distort their understanding of their Lord.

In Acts 10, Peter's triple refusal to eat the unclean things that come down to him in a vision is given a triple reprimand by God. He is told not to call unclean what God has cleansed. Later, at Cornelius' house Peter is amazed when "unclean" Gentiles receive the Spirit of God. Called to account in Jerusalem (Acts 11:1-18), Peter explains his taking of the gospel to Gentiles by telling of the vision, disavowing personal responsibility, and suggesting that objections should be addressed to God. Did Peter learn the truth God brought him in the vision?

In Galatians 2:11-14 we find that Peter was still bound by his Jewish traditions regarding cleanliness (at least when other Jewish Christians were watching). His refusal to eat with Gentiles demeaned their faith, and risked perverting the faith by imposing divisive traditions contrary to the gospel. This time God reprimanded him with the voice of Paul.

All three of these stories about Peter (Matt 16, Acts 10, and Gal 2) reveal a disciple who is a convinced traditionalist. He was so thoroughly committed to his traditions that he allowed them to obscure the truths of the gospel. Peter the disciple had to learn that God has the right to overturn traditions. He had to learn that traditions are less important than people. He had to learn that traditions retained must be channels through which the gospel flows to others, rather than dams that would stagnate the living water of the gospel.

Several years ago the *California Southern Baptist* ran a picture of a small, white, frame building. An enormous sign on the front of the building read, "An Old Fashioned Southern Baptist Church." I do not know what the membership was like. But the sign out front seemed to warn the curious: "If you don't want to be old fashioned and southern and Baptist, don't bother coming in here." Traditions can be valuable. But something is terribly wrong if my traditions become a barrier that reserves the gospel only for those who will first agree to be like me.

One key tradition that Peter had to reexamine was the traditional role of leadership. The first hint the Gospel writers give us about Peter's perspective on leadership is his response to Jesus' chosen role as suffering servant. As already seen, Peter objected. The messiah rules. He doesn't serve.

Peter's objection was more than commentary on the role of the messiah. It was also a reflection of the role he saw for himself as a follower of the messiah. He and the other disciples dreamed of power and prominence. They saw themselves as authoritative figures in the messiah's court in the future kingdom.

In Matthew 20:20-28, we read that the mother of James and John asked that her sons be given the two most prominent places in the kingdom that the messiah would establish. The other disciples (Peter included) did not react as if the question were ignorant. They were angry because James and John asked for the same kind of preeminence that they wanted as well. Jesus dealt with their rivalry by revealing that leaders in his kingdom will not be "tyrants" like the Gentile rulers. Rather, they must be servants like the Son of Man.

Judas' betrayal is explained by some scholars as a last-ditch attempt to force Jesus into a conflict that would result in an earthly kingdom. Was it Judas' desire, from the beginning, to be part of the ruling elite in a powerful new kingdom? Was he frustrated by Jesus' teachings regarding servanthood and suffering for others? Perhaps, in the end, he did indeed reject Jesus because he realized that Jesus would never give him the kingdom and the power he craved. A "disciple" who craves prominence and power will always be disappointed by the results of following Jesus.

On the night of the betrayal, Jesus attempted to wash the feet of his disciples (John 13:1-11). Peter refused. Slaves wash feet. Masters don't. Jesus' stern response to Peter, "Unless I wash you, you have no share with me," drives home the same point that was made when James and John asked for positions of power. In this world rulers dominate and dictate, but such is not to be so among the followers of Jesus. For the one that is greatest among them is to be servant of all.

Did you realize that these are Jesus' only specific statements about leadership in the Gospels? All four Gospel writers considered them significant enough to record. Did the disciples ever understand Jesus' radical redefinition of the meaning of leadership? I think Peter did.

The one whom Jesus instructed, "Tend my sheep" (John 21:16), eventually had the task of instructing others who would be leaders in Christ's church. 1 Peter 5:2-4 indicates that the disciple Peter finally outgrew the natural desire for power and prominence and matured in the faith enough to truly follow Jesus' teaching and example of leadership. The true leader gives himself in service and leads by example. He is not self-serving. His desire is not to dominate. What Peter learned from Jesus, he sought to teach to others who also would serve as Christian leaders:

I exhort the elders among you to tend the flock of God that is in your charge, exercising the oversight, not under compulsion but willingly, as God would have you do it—not for sordid gain but eagerly. Do not lord it over those in your charge, but be examples to the flock. And when the chief shepherd appears, you will win the crown of glory that never fades away. (1 Pet 5:1-4)

The canonical accounts of Peter present us with an example of a disciple who learned to temper self-confidence with humility. Peter's growth as a disciple also required him to learn that people are more important than traditions, and that traditions retained must be traditions that serve the truths of the gospel. Finally, Peter was one who struggled to free himself from his culture's lust for prominence and power, and to become a true follower of a suffering servant.

I do not believe that Peter's story is unique. All too often I catch a reflection of myself while looking at his struggles to become a true follower of Jesus. I can only pray that I, like Peter, will learn well the lessons that transform life and earn the name "disciple." I pray the same for you.

Note

[1]F. V. Filson, "Peter," *Interperter's Dictionary of the Bible*, ed. George Buttrick, 12 vols. (Nashville: Abingdon Press, 1962) 3:757.

†††

An Invitation to Discipleship

Luke 6:27-30

David M. May

In a class on Jesus' portrayal in cinema, I point out to my students that Jesus, the actor, had his first cinematic role in two films that came out in 1916: D. W. Griffith's *Intolerance* and Thomas Ince's *Civilization*.[1] Jesus had his first speaking role in Julien Duvivier's 1935 film *Golgotha;* he spoke French.[2] Since the time of these early films, Jesus' life has been a central theme for movie moguls who see a marketable product, and it continues to hold a fascination for movie-goers who want to experience the Christ event by way of visualization.

Even today when you read the written pages of the New Testament or listen to the public reading of the Gospels, it is similar to watching a movie. Perhaps no Gospel stimulates the celluloid imagination as much as Luke. You can almost sense a movie-crowd's emotions as they would watch and anticipate the parade of Jesus' life from the Gospel of Luke being flashed upon the screen.

In scene one (Chapter one), the crowd cheers the good news of the birth of John the Baptist to a man and woman who never in their wildest dreams could have anticipated a child. It's a happy ending, but it's only the beginning.

In scene two (Chapter two) the crowd cheers again at another birth; this time it is of the star, Jesus. With all the pyrotechnics of the latest Hollywood magic, the sky is filled with the heavenly host and the Dolby Sen-surround reverberates with "Glory to God in the Highest."

In scene three (Chapter three) the crowd witnesses the confirmation of Jesus as God's Son at the Baptism. His Heavenly Father gives him the signal: Go!

In scene four (Chapter four) the crowd draws a deep collective breath as the first conflict enters into the parade of Jesus' life. Jesus becomes tested by the Tempter. Will he fail? Will he surmount the obstacle or succumb to temptation? The good guy wins. A collective sign of relief goes up in the theater. Jesus sends the "Father of Lies" scurrying off the scene, and the crowd can once again settle back into their seats and munch their popcorn.

In scene five (Chapter five) the crowd cheers again as the Jesus parade gathers steam and Jesus picks disciples, amasses a following, and heals a leper.

In scene six (Chapter six) not everyone is an enthusiastic supporter of the Jesus parade. The Pharisees attempt to halt the parade by accusing Jesus when he approaches a man with a withered hand. Yet Jesus, to the movie-goers' delight, with a one liner that stands with the best Clint Eastwoodian phrase says, "Is it lawful on the sabbath to do good or to do harm, to save life or to destroy it?" Dumfounded as the Pharisees are, Jesus has got them.

This movie is wonderful. The movie crowd is enjoying the spectacle that is presented for its viewing pleasure and recommended by all reviewers. Then the unthinkable happens. The film freezes—in midframe—and Jesus steps onto that small ledge between the screen and where the audience is sitting. Of course the Gospel of Luke in 6:17 puts it a little differently. It says Jesus comes to a level spot and stops and begins delivering the Sermon on the Plain.

But for the movie goers, for all of those gathered in that theater expecting the typical fare, there is Jesus standing on that small ledge. His surprise appearance provokes an awkward and uncomfortable feeling. His movie actions that all had cheered and enjoyed vicariously are replaced with just his words, dialogue, but not really dialogue, rather monologue.

He begins to describe qualities, not rules or regulations, but qualities of discipleship that he seeks from all those who only moments ago were passively enjoying the film story, his story. The description is filled with expectations from those who are willing to leave their seats and follow for the rest of the parade. For much of his sermon polite silence reigns, however, it is the type of silence that spawns many thoughts. All is silent until Jesus says:

> But to you who listen I say, love your enemies, do favors for those who hate you, bless those who curse you, pray for your abusers. When someone strikes you on the cheek, offer the other as well. When someone takes away your coat, don't prevent that person from taking your shirt along with it. Give to everyone who begs from you; and when someone takes your things, don't ask for them back. (Luke 6:27-30)[3]

Then a voice from the back of the darkened theater interrupts. "Now wait, that's not the way one should handle a hostile enemy situation. You kill my dog, I'll kill your cat; kill my cat, I'll kill your cow; kill my cow, I'll kill your mule; kill my mule, I'll kill you.[4] Or to put it another way, scratch my car, I'll kick in your fender; kick in my fender, I'll break your windshield; break my windshield; I'll slash your tires."

Jesus' reply to the nameless and remote voice is simple. To join this parade means a discipleship which has no room for unlimited retaliation.[5] To live with this philosophy means that the end of every conflict situations is only mutually assured destruction (MAD).

"Of course," speaks another person from the third row who is fumbling with his pocket Testament, "from the Old Testament it is clear that what God requires of us is an eye for an eye, a tooth for a tooth, a burn for a burn, a car scratch for a car scratch. Do unto another, no more, but also no less than what he or she has done to you."

Jesus' reply to this response once again is simple. Certainly many may practice a type of discipleship that believes that limited retaliation is justice, but in reality it is only a way to get even, to settle scores old and new. Discipleship is more.

"And I know what it is," another voice from a wing of the theater speaks out. Necks craned to hear the wisdom of such an assertive and authoritative voice.

"You are right, to a point, we must love, but one must be careful when, where, and how one loves. If you scratched my car in the church parking lot, well of course, I would forgive you and still love you. But, now if you were out vandalizing on a Sunday morning the cars of good, worshiping people, then you must be taught a lesson. You must be made to pay."

Jesus' reply is to the point. There is no room for two standards of love. You cannot clothe an action in this type of "loving" and call it discipleship; this is a false discipleship. There is not one standard of love for people like us, those who fit into our expectation, and another standard for those outside the group, those who are strangers or even enemies. A greater love is required of a disciple than limited love.

"The way of discipleship is the way of unlimited love." Jesus' words cut through the silence of the theater as the crowd leans forward to catch the words. "It is love that continues to act lovingly even when someone takes advantage of you. The discipleship I seek is the love that surprises both the love-receiver and the love-giver. It surprises the thief by giving a shirt to go with the stolen coat. It surprises the beggar by wrapping a bill within a hand. It surprises those who take our possessions by demanding nothing back. It surprises you when you give love out to those who treat you as any enemy."

"Why is it that 'good' people have missed grasping this quality of discipleship and yet Hollywood has occasionally gotten it right?"

"Have you seen the movie *The Mission?*" A wave of the heads nodded in the theater.

"It is the story of a small paradisiacal Catholic mission in South America during the eighteenth century. It is a mission populated by natives, beautiful people, who carry within themselves a spirit of God that defies definition, yet this spirit manifests itself in music and love for one another. Two priests live out their ministries in the mission, Gabriel (Jeremey Irons) who in coming in peace and love had brought the gospel message to these natives, and Mendoza (Robert De Niro), a solider, who had only recently given up the sword for the way of peace and love.

"Conflict is brought into the story when the mission is threatened by the expansion of the Portuguese and Spanish slave trade. The slave traders, the enemies, stand ready to invade the mission and in a climactic scene the two priests argue about taking up the sword to defend the mission: Mendoza for, Gabriel against. Mendoza argues persuasively that to save the innocent lives of the sweet natured natives, the blood of the invaders must be spilled. The greater good must be served. After all his arguments Gabriel makes this one poignant statement, a statement of surprise, 'If might be right, then where in the world is there room for love'."

"Be on your guard against a form of discipleship that dilutes and weakens the unlimited love of enemies, that softens your actions when struck upon the cheek. One must be careful not to succumb to the false discipleship slogans of expediency and the slogans of the time: 'War is sometimes necessary,' 'Peace through strength,' 'They got what they deserved' and 'The end justifies the means.' Seek to surprise with love. Discipleship is to catch off guard your neighbor and your enemy by giving love."

Jesus paused.

"As you sit in this theater, you are thinking. No doubt you can raise many objections. You might say that this way of discipleship was okay for the day and age of the Bible and the first disciples. In their world they could love enemies, turn the other cheek, pray for those who abused, but it won't work today. You think, be pragmatic. Our world is a complicated and complex place, we are global in how we relate to others. Our behaviors are dictated by policy, contracts, and good sense. But the world in which the first disciples walked was also complicated and complex. It is no more or less hard to love an enemy today than it was two thousand years ago.

"You might be contemplating the implications when you truly begin to live out discipleship. What is the cost of discipleship when one loves like this? In the movie *The Mission*, with the invasion of the slave traders imminent, Gabriel begins a surprising action. He sets up a table and upon it he places bread and wine and, the priests and natives begin to celebrate. While the natives and priest are participating in the Supper, no miracles happen, no angels intervene, no rescue. Instead, the inevitable happens. The slave traders with chains and guns burst upon the scene, destruction and massacre occur; the priest Gabriel dies.

"The next to the last scene in *The Mission* is that of a Cardinal ensconced safely in the Church's headquarters as he receives news of the death of his priest and the end of the mission by the slave traders. The news was not a total surprise since he had condoned the action and by his inactivity condemned them to their fate. The Cardinal gazed out of a window in the direction of the setting sun and uttered the pained words: 'All my priests are dead, but I am alive, but actually they are alive and I am dead'.

"No one person, no group of people, no nation, no law can put out the fire, the light, and the life of true discipleship. The weapon of the spirit, the ability to surprise by and through the action of love, will always conquer. Ridicule, obstacles, persecution, and even death cannot stand against those who follow in discipleship."

Jesus stopped. We held our breath.

Then Jesus spoke for one last time, "Come, join the parade of discipleship. Fold up your chairs, put down the cokes and popcorn, and participate, don't just watch from the audience. Lay aside your jackets, put away your ticket stubs and receipts. Lay aside anything that holds you back and come. You know at least a bit about what you can expect on the way when you join and when you love."

It's outrageous to think that a cinematic Jesus could or would step from a screen and issue an invitation for movie goers to participate in discipleship—a discipleship of unlimited love and all that is entails. Perhaps it's outrageous to believe that a story from the Bible can leap off of the page and so grab and possess you that you make a decision to follow on a path of discipleship. It's not only outrageous; it's wonderful when it happens.

Notes

¹Michael Singer, "Cinema Savior," *Film Comment* (October, 1988): 44.
²Ibid., 45.
³Robert J. Miller, ed. *The Complete Gospels: Annotated Scholars Version* (Sonoma CA: Polebridge Press, 1992) 131.
⁴Clarence Jordan, *Sermon on the Mount* (Valley Forge PA: Judson Press, 1952) 64.
⁵The following four ways of approaching the world are presented in Clarence Jordan's book listed above, 63-71.

†††

Following Jesus
Parts I & II

1 Peter 2:21; Mark 8:34-36;
Nehemiah 8:1-3, 9-10

H. Stephen Shoemaker

Part I

The minister was preparing his sermon for the next day in his study at home. The text was 1 Peter 2:21:

> For to this you have been called, because Christ also suffered for you, leaving you an example, so that you should follow in his steps.

The sermon theme was to be "Following in Jesus' Steps." As Henry Maxwell worked on the sermon the doorbell rang. He opened the door and there stood a rather shabby looking man looking for work. The minister said he was sorry he had no work to give him—and sent him on his way. Then he returned to the study and finished the sermon.

The next day at the First Church he delivered the sermon masterfully. The congregation nodded its approval. The worship service was as well put together as the congregation was well-dressed. Everything was going in perfect order when it happened. The same shabbily dressed man came down the aisle and began a speech to the congregation.

He told them that he'd been laid off work for ten months and had ever since been wandering from city to city looking for work.

He spoke directly, without any tone of condemnation but with a question that was inescapable:

> I've tramped through this city for three days trying to find a job; and in all that time I've not had a word of sympathy or comfort except from your minister here, who said he was sorry for me and hoped I would find a job somewhere. I suppose it is because you get so imposed upon by the professional tramp that you have lost interest in any other sort. . . . Of course, I understand you can't go out of your way to hunt up jobs for other people like me. I'm not asking you to; but what I feel puzzled about is, what is meant by following Jesus. What do you mean when you sing, "I'll go with Him, with Him, all the way."

He said a few more words then he collapsed on the floor. The pastor had him carried to his home where he could rest for a few days and regain his strength. During the week while staying at the parsonage to everyone's great shock the man died.

The next Sunday Henry Maxwell got up to preach, a man deeply shaken by the events of the week. The man's question "What do you mean by following Jesus?" was driven so deeply into the minister's heart that it put a question mark over everything in the minister's life and work.

So when he stood there before the congregation he confessed his shakiness and made a proposal:

> I want volunteers from the First Church who will pledge themselves earnestly and honestly for an entire year not to do anything without first asking the question, What would Jesus do? and after asking the question, each one will follow Jesus exactly as he knows how, no matter what the result will be. I will, of course, include myself in this company of volunteers, and shall take for granted that my church here will not be surprised at my future conduct, as based upon this standard of action.

Maxwell invited all who would respond to join him at the close of the service to discuss the plan. "Our motto will be 'What would Jesus do?' Our aim will be to act just as He would if He was in our places, regardless of immediate results."[1]

He offered the plan. A core group responded and the church and community were over the course of the next year profoundly changed. Among the group was the editor of the city's paper, the owner of a business, a housewife, a music teacher. The question raised the deepest possible issues for everyone in the group. This experiment in discipleship had two essential requirements: (1) the time commitment of one year; and (2) the mutual support and guidance of the small group of volunteers who pledged to meet weekly.

I.

You may have recognized the story by now. It is Charles Sheldon's 1896 novel and spiritual classic, *In His Steps*. It was to the social gospel movement in America what Charles Dicken's novels were to the social reform movement in Victorian England. Many of you may have read it. I read it as a twenty-year-old and thought it was a nice book. Not long ago as one who had turned forty, I read it again and experienced it as a profound and affecting and immensely helpful book. I also discovered it was a book about a mid-life crisis of a minister. It seems every book I read these days is about mid-life crises. Funny.

When I re-read Sheldon's classic, it felt like a new book. The simplicity of the question drove straight home to my heart and it sounded like good news. What would Jesus do. It is not a simplistic question. Sometimes it is a haunting one. Flannery O'Connor said somewhere that the South is not so much Christ-centered as it is Christ-haunted. The question is not as easy as it sounds but I cannot imagine going anywhere with Jesus without starting there. It is a question that examines everything in our lives, one that brings trouble as well as help, but when I heard that question in the new reading of the old book, it cut through the complexity of my life and sounded for all the world like good news. What would Jesus do? It sounded like the simplicity that lies on the yonder side of complexity—not the simplistic answers that lie this side of complexity but the spiritual gift noted by saints of the simplicity that lies on the yonder side.

There are times of great spiritual opportunity in our lives and in the life of a congregation. Times when we are faced with almost overwhelming challenge and opportunity for good. Like today. Times of expanding responsibility—which may be used for good or for ill. Times like mid-life when unmet needs and unanswered questions build a great pressure within and you search for a way to live "Christianly" in the storm of it all. Or times when life has dragged a painful plowshare across the surface of your life and now you are ready as never before to receive the seed of God's word, receive it with joy. Times of vocational choice or vocational disruption. Times of illness. Times of crisis.

There are times when the Spirit of God "digs out our ears," to use a painfully concrete biblical metaphor, and we can hear again, and our hearts are opened and lights are turned on inside our heads. And we find ourselves almost despite ourselves following Christ in a new and fresh way.

When a new pastor comes to a new congregation, it is an opportunity for both to hear something new and do something new, to say "Don't be surprised by my behavior, I'm trying to follow Jesus." We may be surprised. I hope so.

II.

The Old Testament reading is a deeply moving one to me. Jerusalem and Temple had been destroyed and the Hebrew people taken into captivity. Exile had disrupted regular worship and hearing of God's word. Many in Jerusalem had not heard God's word in a long time, some perhaps never.

Now exile is over and Jerusalem is being rebuilt. Ezra, the priest, is asked to stand and read from God's word, the Torah.

When Ezra began to read people began to weep. Why? Was it out of guilt or shame? Had they wandered far away from the path and only now recognized how far? Was it a weeping for joy? After so long a silence they heard the beloved words again. Can you imagine not hearing scripture for years, then one day a voice begins to read aloud:

The Lord is my shepherd I shall not want. . . .

For God so loved the world that He gave his only begotten son. . . .

Come let us reason together, saith the Lord,
    though your sins are as scarlet I shall make them white as snow.

Come unto me ye who are weary and heavy laden.

When the people heard Ezra read they began to weep. Nehemiah spoke to the people's weeping: "This day is holy to the Lord your God; do not mourn or weep. Go your way, eat the fat things and drink sweet wine and send portions to those who have none; for this day is holy to the Lord; Do not be grieved, for the joy of the Lord is your strength."

That's what happened when Jesus came, and wherever the gospel is heard. The bridegroom, the feast, the joy of the Lord our strength. Any new hearing of God's word, any new attempt of discipleship, is bound to be mixed with some sorrow or remorse over the past and with no little apprehension about the future—will I try and fail once again? Oh, my loyal flaws.

But God tells us to rise and shine! This is a holy day, a day of feasting and rejoicing. "For the joy of the Lord is your strength."

So the question comes. Will you join this quest, a new quest to follow Jesus, to attempt as never before to follow in His steps? I will join you.

It is a little scary to take such a step; you don't know where it will end. Do not be afraid. God will not ask anything of you that is not for your healing and at the same time the healing of the world. Christ's call calls forth your joy and turns you to a world in need. It should sound like good news. It may be painful and difficult but down deep you know it is good news—just like the surgeon's words "We can operate" sometimes come as great good news. You should not answer any call as God's call until and unless it feels like good news. Christ's call to follow should bring a rising joy and a sense of grand adventure.

And he said to Peter and Andrew, "Follow me and I will make you fishers of men, women, and men." And they immediately rose and followed.

"Leave the dead to bury the dead and come follow me."

And Jesus saw a man named Matthew setting at the tax office; and he said, "Follow me."

And he said, "If anyone would come after me, let them deny themselves and take up their cross daily and follow me."

"One thing you still lack. Sell all that you have and give to the poor and you will have treasure in heaven; and come follow me."

The next day Jesus decided to go to Galilee and he found Philip and said to him, "Follow me."

"My sheep hear my voice, and I know them, and they follow me; and I give them eternal life."

"If anyone serves me, he/she, must follow me; and where I am, there shall my servant be also."

When they had finished breakfast, Jesus said to Simon Peter, "Simon, son of John, do you love me more than these?" "Yes, Lord; you know that I love you." "Feed my lambs." "Simon, son of John, do you love me?" "Yes, Lord, you know that I love you." "Tend my sheep." "Simon, son of John, do you love me?" "Lord, you know everything; you know that I love you." "Feed my sheep." And after this he said, "Follow me."

When we appear before Christ on the day of judgment, he will stand and show us his nail scarred hands and we will not be afraid. For the One who is Judge is the same as the One who died for us. And he'll not ask about Southern or Baptist or Presbyterian or verbal plenary inspiration or vicarious substitutionary atonement; he'll ask, "Did you follow me? Go with me? Feed my sheep? Did you love my appearing . . . and love the least of these? Did you let me love the world through you?"

So today will you answer the call anew, maybe for the first time, to walk in His steps? To ask more often: What would Jesus do? and follow where that leads no matter the results.

Where to begin? For now where we begin is with the desire to begin, a deep willingness to follow that is itself a work of the Holy Spirit. E. Stanley Jones was asked once what it meant to become a Christian. He answered:

> To give as much of yourself as you can to as much of Christ as you know.[2]

I think that is a step any of us can take today. Tomorrow you may be able to give more and tomorrow you may know more of Christ to give yourself to. But anyone here this day can take this step: to give as much of yourself as you can to as much of Christ as you know. Would you?

Part II

In the sermon entitled "Following Jesus" I spoke of the spiritual project that Henry Maxwell put before his congregation in Charles Sheldon's classic, *In His Steps*. A street person showed up at church asked what it meant to follow Jesus, collapsed and later that week died. Things got down to basics as the pastor and church were shaken by the event. The pastor challenged the congregation to not make any decision for one year without first asking, "What would Jesus do?" And to follow regardless of the results. The ones who joined the project pledged to meet together to give each other support and guidance. A small group of volunteers came forward and for a year met every week. Profound changes happened to them and to the congregation.

The book upon a re-reading in forty's something mid-life was a deeply moving one to me. The simplicity of the question cut through the complexity of my life and sounded for all the world like good news.

Christ's call should sound like good news. If it doesn't, wait and see if it is truly good news before you act. Decisions to follow Christ may be difficult and painful but down deep you know they are good news. Christ's call is always for your healing and for the healing of the world. It calls forth joy and turns you to a world in need. The character of true discipleship is a following that is glad and free. Not coerced, guilty, obliging, but glad and free.

Christ calls you to follow with your true self, a following that is glad and free.

So relax and follow. Here are some guidelines. Five. Not Ten Commandments, Five Guidances.

I.

Begin to ask the question, "What would Jesus do?" before making decisions. This is no simplistic question. There are no easy automatic answers, but I do not think we can go anywhere with Jesus without first asking that question.

This may involve a more literal following of Jesus than you have let yourself consider before. It may involve a more radical step of discipleship than you have ever taken. Perhaps you have wanted to take it before, but you have not been sure what it was the first step was, or it has not been the right time, or you have just not had it in you to do it. The one who calls you dwells in you and gives you the power to follow.

To ask the question and discern the answer involves an act of holy imagination. This is where the Holy Spirit comes to our aid. It requires an act of the human imagination to jump from what Jesus said and did in first century Palestine to what he might do today. But God has sent the Spirit to be our teacher, our translator of Christ's way from first century language and action to language and action of today.

This following involves our attitudes as well as our actions. Following Jesus is not just going where he goes and doing what he does but also "having the mind among you that was in Christ Jesus." Letting His mind and heart interpenetrate with ours so that we think His thoughts and feel His feelings and "attitude" His attitude.

First, begin to ask more often, "What would Jesus do?"

II

The second guidance comes from Mother Theresa. Henri Nouwen once asked her in Calcutta, "How do I live out my vocation as a priest?" She answered,

> Spend one hour a day in adoration of your Lord and never do anything you know is wrong and you will be alright.[3]

I think that is a beautifully simple guide for us all in our vocation as Christian disciples.

Step two is: *Spend one hour a day in adoration of our Lord.*

We don't have to spend the hour in sixty consecutive minutes. That is not the most fruitful path for everyone. The hour may begin as we rise and wake and say the words, "This is the day the Lord hath made. Let one rejoice and be glad in it." Adoration of the Lord through the beauty of a sunrise or sunset or a painting or a piece of music can be true prayer if we see the Lord behind it all.

Adoration of Christ involves some actual contact with His words. So you need somewhere in the day to open to those New Testament Gospels and read some of Christ's words and read of His life.

We probably spend more time every day learning the mind of Phil Donahue or Oprah Winfrey or Rush Limbaugh or Ellen Goodman or George Will or Molly Ivins or Gary Trudeau or Calvin and Hobbs or Paul Harvey or George Strait or the Grateful Dead (have I gotten everybody?) than we do learning the mind of Christ. So start the day or end the day or take ten minutes during the day to open a gospel and read a paragraph, to reflect and pray upon it.

I have a suggestion to jump start your new beginnings at discipleship, your new learning of and following of Christ. Take a couple of hours one day and read through the Gospel of Mark in one sitting. Mark is the shortest, most action-packed Gospel and it can be done. I find that the newer translations that break the Gospel into paragraphs rather than just verses and often put headings on the paragraphs aid in such reading.

Lastly, spend some time, if only a few minutes each day, alone in simple adoration of Christ. Alone, with no distractions. No books, no music, alone. The true self needs to be free from all external distractions and influences so that it can be alone with itself and with God. This may be in the car with no radio on, beside your bed, an early morning walk, at your desk before the onslaught begins.

Guidance number two: spend one hour a day in adoration of your Lord.

III.

Mother Theresa said, "Spend one hour a day in adoration of your Lord and never do anything you know is wrong and you will be alright." Guidance Three: *"Never do anything you know is wrong."*

You may laugh and say that is fine for Mother Theresa to say but I am not Mother Theresa. But her words are not a demand for perfection. She does not say, "Never do anything wrong," but "Never do anything you know is wrong." (Even that seems like a stretch!)

We will do wrong. Sometimes we do not know 'til later on that what we've been doing is wrong. We need the Spirit in us to know that. Our minds are hungry to rationalize, our hearts deceive us. Only Word and Spirit lead us to the truth. The point is, when you discover what you are doing is wrong to stop the behavior. That is easier to say than to do, but the only way to stop is to stop. Ask God's help and stop.

Mother Theresa's words are helpful because they help to free us from a life of inner conflict when we are knowingly, continuously doing what we know inside to be wrong. That inner conflict will wear us out and wear us down.

Sometimes the guilt itself paralyzes us and keeps us from changing. Sometimes we live in shame. Healthy guilt says, "You made a mistake." Unhealthy shame says, "You are a mistake." Healthy guilt says, "This is sin." Unhealthy shame says: "You are no good, worthless."

God wants us to be able to acknowledge our wrongs, receive forgiveness, start the healing process, and get on.

You cannot follow Christ unhinderedly when you are doing things you know are wrong. Your soul and spirit and mind and body are compromised. I use the word "compromised" in a medical sense, not in a shame-making moral sense. To have something in your body compromised means there is something happening that keeps it from working at peak efficiency. A heart with damaged muscle is compromised. It will need to learn to compensate and rebuild.

A life that is doing what it knows is wrong is compromised. It cannot be functioning at its best. Christ wants for us a life that is fruitful, that is glad and free and functioning at its best.

I pray for you an unhindered following of Christ, one joyful and free, increasing in the love of God and neighbor. Avoiding what you know is wrong, stopping what you know is wrong is an important step.

IV.

The fourth guidance is this: Spend *time every week in corporate worship and group Bible study.* We cannot adequately worship or study alone. We need one another to help us worship and learn. We need each other for encouragement and to keep each other honest.

One of the lessons of *In His Steps* was the weekly get together of those who made the pledge. They needed each other to talk through how they were trying to answer "What would Jesus do?"

It is important to spend time alone with the Lord and with scripture. Guidance number two acknowledges this. It honors the principle of soul competency and soul freedom and priesthood of the believers. It helps us avoid spiritual tyranny and "group-think" and give us opportunity to hear Christ's voice above all other voices. But we also need *corporate* worship so that we learn better how to praise God and confess our sins and pray and listen to scripture and offer ourselves. And we need community Bible study so we can learn from one another and so our friends can keep us honest.

We discover best how to be Christian in *community.* We need each other. That is why Christ established a church. We human persons are social creatures; we learn and grow and are nourished in community.

So step four, spend time weekly in corporate worship and group Bible study. This is the singular importance of Sunday morning Sunday school and worship.

V.

Fifth, *get your **body** involved in some kind of ministry with people.* Prayerfully consider how you will give of your time, talents, and resources and act. Act now. Act even before you think you are ready. I am speaking of changes in life experiences and weekly patterns that will issue into changes within, changes in feelings and faith. I remember the answer Gerard Manley Hopkins gave a man who wrote saying he was in a faith crisis and wondered what advice this mystic poet would give. Hopkins wrote back a two word answer: Give alms.[4]

Christ calls everyone of us to get involved with people for His Sake, in His Name. He calls us to love people nobody else will love, to make a difference in our society from the lowest to the highest rungs.

What most of us need is not a change in theology, but a change in our lives and life patterns. We need new experiences, experiences that happen as we take risks, get involved, do new things for Christ, building Habitat houses, making a verbal witness for Christ, teaching fourth-grade boys, changing diapers in the Lord.

Prayerfully consider how you will give yourself and act. Don't act apart from prayer. Don't pray and fail to act.

There they are, five guidances:

Ask the question, "What would Jesus do?"
Spend an hour everyday in adoration of your Lord.
Never do anything you know is wrong.
Commit weekly to corporate worship and group Bible study.
Get your body involved in some kind of ministry.

Christ's promise to us is that as we follow him he abides in us. May his grace empower you and may you who follow walk in beauty and peace.

Notes

[1]Charles Sheldon, *In His Steps* (New York: Grosset and Dunlap, n.d.) 9ff.
[2]The original source of this well-known quote is unknown.
[3]Henry Nouwen, *The Way of the Heart* (New York: Seabury Press, 1981) 31.
[4]The original source is unknown.

†††

Look Again

Matthew 5:21-48

R. Wayne Stacy

"Cognitive dissonance." It's a term often used in contemporary parlance, especially in psychological and educational disciplines. It's kind of strange in that it's a "feeling term" that takes out a loan from the "bank of intellect." It means the ambivalence and confusion that you often feel when expectation collides with experiences. I remember, when I was a kid, there was this TV program about a family marooned in space. It was appropriately called *Lost in Space*, and my favorite character on the program was the family's robot who, when difficult situations arose, would roll around on his caterpillar trace feet, waving his arms wildly in the air and shouting "that does not compute!" Cognitive dissonance.

I remember the first time cognitive dissonance made a real "impression," shall we say, on me. I was in the sixth grade. It happened when my Christian faith and ethics in which I had been scrupulously reared ran smack up against Joe Goode—G·O·O·D·E. He was not. Joe was a big, rangey, blonde-haired boy from Michigan who towered over most of the other sixth grade boys, including me. His parents were migrant workers who followed the winter vegetable harvest to South Florida every year and, consequently, Joe had seen the tougher side of life, adding to the mystique that gathered around him.

It was "recess," as we used to call it, and we were playing football, a game in most places, but a religion in Florida. I had been brought up in church and had been taught the Christian ethic by my parents and Sunday School teachers. "Turn the other cheek," had been part of the moral fabric out of which my own emerging ethical system was being fashioned, and my older brother's "spin" on that commandment, "Love your enemies; it'll drive them crazy!" seemed for all the world like sound advice.

But right there on the playground, cognitive dissonance sprang up and assaulted me! In a dispute between Joe and me, over what now I cannot even remember, Joe threatened to "punch my lights out." Everyone gathered around, including Mr. Threlkeld, our teacher, to see the show. Joe put up his fists and walked around me in a threatening posture.

I said—and Mr. Morrison, my Beginners Sunday School teacher would have been proud of me—"Joe, fighting doesn't solve anything. I'm sure we can work this out without fighting. Besides, I'm a Christian; I don't believe in fighting."

Well, with that there was an audible "Ahhhh" from the blood-thirsty little savages who had gathered to watch the brawl. But Joe, who apparently missed the "turn the other cheek" lesson in Sunday School, promptly smacked me right in the mouth. I was more shocked than hurt. Later, wiping the blood from my mouth, the cognitive dissonance set in. "What good is it to 'turn the other cheek' if you're the only one playing this game?" I thought. Haven't they heard about the Sermon on the Mount in Michigan?

That was my first real experience with "cognitive dissonance," when the utter impracticality of the Sermon on the Mount was "impressed" on me by Joe Goode, but it was not to be my last. And more than once, the Sermon on the Mount proved to be the culprit.

When I was about fourteen, I figured out what Matthew 5:29 was really talking about; you know, "If your right eye offend you, pluck it out and throw it away." I was about to be in trouble, big time, when I discovered General Psychology and found out, just in the nick of time, that it was utterly unrealistic anyway to expect a normal adolescent to use his eyes only for doing homework! What a relief it was to learn that psychology had given me "permission" to look, every now and again, with a "lustful eye." It's a big word in some psychological circles, "permission."

And, in a way, that's what I did with the rest of the Sermon on the Mount, too. Did you?

I mean, have you read this stuff? Not only is murder wrong, but anger! Not only is adultery a "no no," but lust! And if someone smacks you in the mouth on the playground you're supposed to say: "C'mon now; you can do better than that!"

What a relief it was when my psychology professors gave me cogent sounding explanations for my anger and lust and penchant to retaliate. "After all, you're only human. And anger and lust and good ole healthy self-interest are the stuff of humanity. Don't be so hard on yourself!" Or as the young people would say: "Get real!" That's the problem, isn't it? The Sermon on the Mount just isn't very realistic, not in our kind of world. I mean, "it's a jungle out there!"

I was comforted again when, in seminary, I learned that even the Bible scholars had trouble taking the Sermon on the Mount seriously. Martin Luther, as early as the 16th century, threw up his hands and said, "You can't live like this, not in our kind of world!" And so, he devised a more realistic interpretation of the Sermon. "Two Kingdoms," he called it. "You see," he said, "there are these two kingdoms in which the Christian finds himself/herself—the kingdom of this world in which it is totally impractical to attempt to live what the Sermon teaches, and then there is the Kingdom of God, the new world that God is bringing, in which it will then be possible to live out the Sermon. Until that world comes, we should embrace the demands of the Sermon in our hearts, but to try to carry out those demands in our day to day lives now just isn't very practical."

Albert Schweitzer also offered a "realistic" interpretation of the Sermon. Schweitzer, noticing that Jesus spoke a lot about a "coming age" and attempting to take seriously the eschatological nature of Jesus's message, suggested that the ethical demands in the Sermon on the Mount constitute an "interim ethic." That is, Jesus' demands were addressed to his disciples as a way to live in the "time between the times," when God would send his messiah to bring about a New World. But, of course, Schweitzer thought that Jesus never believed himself to be that messiah and so when Jesus died on the cross in an attempt to force God's hand in bringing this New World, nothing more significant than a good, but misguided Jewish radical died that day, and the Sermon on the Mount, like most of what Jesus had said and taught, was relegated to the dusty annals of first-century Jewish history.

Not one scholar has offered a serious interpretation of the Sermon! Well, one has—Dietrich Bonhöffer. His book, *The Cost of*

Discipleship is a study of discipleship in three parts, the second of which is an interpretation of the Sermon on the Mount that attempts to take what Jesus says with chilling seriousness. He was hanged for trying to take Jesus seriously.

"You have heard it said by Jesus not to resist the one who is evil, but I say to you that you had better look out for number one, if you know what's good for you!" Give them an inch, they'll take a mile. After all, doesn't the Bible say somewhere: "God helps those who help themselves?" You'd better look again before turning the other cheek. Look again before going that second mile. Look again before giving to him who asks. Look again, because how you look makes all the difference in the world!

That's what Jesus is arguing for, really—a different way of looking. That's why he says: "You have heard that it has been said . . . but I say unto you." The scholars call these statements Jesus' "Antitheses" because he is calling for a radically different perspective from his followers.

A lawyer who was asked how she could tell whether or not her clients were lying to her said: "Well, it's a little sad, but I started out with the assumption that everyone who comes to me is lying. I've learned the hard way that usually they are. Then, if I discover that they're telling the truth, I'm pleasantly surprised!" Expect the worst and you'll only rarely be disappointed.

Jesus, however, calls for another way. "everyone who looks at a woman [or a man for that matter] lustfully has already committed adultery with her/him in their hearts." Do you see what He means? By "lust" Jesus does not mean the normal and quite healthy psychological and biological urges; rather, He means to treat another person as though that one were only a thing to be used for our own amusement and purposes. To "thingize" someone is what Jesus is talking about.

In Forrest Carter's *The Education of Little Tree*, there's a remarkable exchange between Little Tree and his Granma on this very thing. In trying to teach Little Tree how to value things properly, Little Tree's Granma said:

> "Little Tree, everybody has two minds. One of the minds has to do with the necessaries for body living. You use it to figure

how to get shelter and eating and such like for the body." "But you also have another mind that has noting' atall to do with such as that," she said, "it's the spirit mind."

She said: "If you only use the body-living mind to think greedy or mean; if you was always cuttin' at folks with it or figuring how to material profit off'n them . . . then you'll shrink up your spirit mind to a size no bigger'n a hickor'nut. And when you die, the body mind dies with you only the spirit-mind goes on livin,' and if you only think with your body mind all your life, there you'll be, stuck with a hickor'nut spirit!"

"You see, Little Tree," she said, "that's how you become dead people, really. You don't just have to be dead in your body to be dead people; all you have to do is let your spirit mind shrink up to the size of a hickor'nut!"

"Dead people! They're easy to spot," she said. "When people look at a woman and see only dirty; when they look at other people and see nothin' but bad; when they look at a tree and see nothin' but lumber and profit, they're just dead people walkin' around!"[1]

Someone strikes you on the cheek, some Roman soldier comes up and commands you to take his backpack—what do you see? Is it even a person that you see? Or would you like, just for a minute, to become the Terminator? Look again! Because how you look makes all the difference in the world!

And sometimes it works, this different way of looking. A few years ago, when I was on the faculty of Midwestern seminary in Kansas City, I was invited to Chilicothe, Missouri to conduct a regional January Bible Study clinic for the Missouri Baptist Convention. One of the participants arrived late, after I had already started. His body language said, "I don't want to be here, and I don't like you."

When we reached a natural breaking point in the presentation and I asked for questions, several pastors in the audience asked good questions and some good dialogue ensued. Then, in a tone of voice that sounded more like he was talking to a tax examiner than a seminary professor, the unwilling participant belligerently asked several questions that were more statements of his total disregard for what I had been saying than they were requests for

information. Looking around for a question in there I could respond to, I tried to answer him as best I could.

When we broke for lunch, I made a beeline for him and sat
down beside him to eat. He look rather sheepishly at me and said:
"I hope you didn't think I was angry with you by my comments."

I said: "No, I've never met you before today, and I'm fairly
confident that I've done nothing to merit your anger. But you are
angry, and I would like to talk with you about it!"

He was so disarmed by my honesty that he sat back, swal-
lowed hard and told me about the pain he had brought with him
into that room that day that had nothing whatever to do with the
Bible Study I was leading. And a friendship was born out of that
encounter that continues still!

Sometimes it works!

But, sometimes it doesn't. Martin Luther King, Jr., treated Bull
Connors in an open and loving way, and Connors beat his head in
with a club.

Hear me. I am not saying that we should try Jesus' way
because it works. Turn the other cheek, go the second mile, return
good for evil, and things will go better for you. NO! Jesus never
says "Turn the other cheek" because it works; He says "turn the
other cheek" because it's right. "Your conduct is not to be determined by how the other treats you; your conduct is determined by
your Father in heaven who sends his rain to fall on the just and
the unjust and causes his sun to shine on the good and the evil."

You want it straight? When Luke is giving his version of all
this he summarizes it with what is, no doubt, the most radical
statement in the New Testament: "God is kind to the ungrateful
and the selfish."

Look again! Neither our friends nor our enemies dictate our
ethics. We are called to be *God's people!* We are called to look at
everyone and everything with the eyes of Christ! No excuses. No
exceptions.

In a little book called *City Streets, City People*, Michael Chris-
tensen tells of his experiences of living and working with Mother
Teresa and her sisters who work among the "poorest of the poor."
The overpopulation, the poverty, and the cruel caste system make
Calcutta a place of unparalleled human misery. The poor of

Calcutta are the "forgotten poor," except for Mother Teresa and
her sisters.. They literally pick up the dying out of the gutters of
Calcutta and nurse them back to health, if possible; and if not, they
give them the grace of a place where they are cared for and loved
in which to die.

He had only been in Calcutta a few weeks before he had come
to realize that he has seen enough "blood and ooze," as he puts it,
to last a lifetime. He confessed that he never dreamed that such
human misery and degradation existed and the constant depression of living with disease, abject poverty, and death had taken its
toll on him. Just the day before—can I tell you this?—he had been
with Mother Teresa as they picked up a child out of the gutter
with no hands and feet. They had been eaten off by rats as the
child lay dying.

One morning, just after mass, when he felt he could take no
more, he confessed to Mother Teresa just how he felt about what
he had seen and experienced.

"How can you live like this day after day? How can you look
in the faces of those hopeless wretches, knowing that the most you
can possibly do to ease their suffering is to help them to die in
peace, with some semblance of human dignity, and then wake up
morning after morning and go out there to face it all over again?"

She said: "Michael, did you see Jesus, today?"

Christensen thought: "I could not truthfully say that I had. All
I saw was suffering, disease, and death. I was simply trying to find
the courage to expose myself to subhuman conditions and cope
with my emotional shock."

And so, he stammered out, "See Jesus? What do you mean?"

Mother Teresa said: "When we love the poor, we do not first
see the poor; first we see Jesus! We are not social workers. We are
minister of Christ's love. What we do, we do for Jesus! And when
we pick up a body off the street and nurture him back to health,
we do it to Jesus. It is His face we see in the faces of the poorest
of the poor!"

Christensen went on to say: "As we sat on the bench outside
the chapel, Mother Teresa took my hand in hers and said:
'Michael, the gospel of Jesus Christ is written on your fingers.' She

slowly pointed to each of my five fingers and said, carefully emphasizing each word, 'You-did-it-to-me'."

"Then, she brought my five fingers together and said: 'See the five wounds of Jesus?' " And Christensen said: "I thought about the two wounds in his hands, the two in his feet, and the one in his side. Then, putting my pointed fingers into the palm of my hand, she said softly: 'This is His love for you'."

" 'Now close your fist,' she said. 'This is the sacred heart of Jesus that says to us: I was hungry, and you gave me to eat; I was thirsty, and you gave me to drink; I was a stranger, and you took me in; I was naked, and you clothed me; I was sick, and you came to me; I was in the gutter, and you picked me up!' "

"And then she said softly: 'At the end of your life, your five fingers will either excuse you or accuse you have having done it to the least of these. You-did-it-to-me!' "[2]

We are called to be God's people, to look at everything and everyone with the eyes of Christ; to live the Sermon not because it works, but because it's right! No excuses. No exceptions.

I know. I know. That's a tall order. Seems impractical. Seems impossible. Creates a little "cognitive dissonance" when you first look at it doesn't it?

But, look again! Look carefully. Because how you look makes all the difference in the world. Isn't that true?[3]

Notes

[1]Forest Carter, *The Education of Little Tree*, reprint. (Albuquerque NM: University of New Mexico Press, 1986) 59-60.

[2]Michael Christensen, *City Streets, City People*. (Nashville TN: Abingdon Press, 1988) 38-39.

[3]Acknowledgement is hereby given to William H. Willimon, "A Second Look," *Preaching* (March-April, 1988): 23-25, from which some of the inspiration for this sermon was taken.

†††

An Affirmation of Faith

Revelation 1:5–6

Jon M. Stubblefield

I was a member of the debate team during college. As we traveled
to a tournament one weekend, a fellow debater turned to me and
said, "I understand you are planning to be a Baptist minister." I
replied, "Yes, this is what I believe God wants me to do with my
life." My friend was quiet for a moment, then he dropped this
bombshell: "Would you mind telling me what you believe and
why?" After recovering from shock, I spent the next hour or so
sharing my affirmation of faith—about God, the Bible, creation,
Jesus Christ, sin, salvation, the church, the Christian life, and
eschatology. It is important for each of us to know what we
believe and why.

Revelation 1:5-6 sets forth a profound affirmation of faith about
the person and work of Jesus Christ. We speak of this text in the
same breath with other great christological passages, such as John
1:1-18, Philippians 2:5-11, and Colossians 1:15-20. Our understanding of Jesus Christ serves as the foundation for Christian
discipleship.

Recall the setting of Revelation. John the apostle had been
exiled to the rugged, lonely island of Patmos, a rocky piece of real
estate in the Aegean Sea used to banish political prisoners. John
was there "on account of the word of God and the testimony of
Jesus" (Rev 1:9).[1] Most likely, Domitian was on the throne in
Rome. He ruled from AD 81–96. By this time emperor worship had
made inroads as the state religion. Christians, however, refused to
declare, "Caesar is Lord." As a result, many suffered for their
convictions, and John was no exception. This faithful apostle had
witnessed the development of Christianity from a fragile
movement to a force so powerful world leaders were threatened
by it. The church was experiencing the heavy hand of persecution.

Believers desperately needed a message of encouragement and hope.

In light of the circumstances, John might have folded his hands and given up. He might have drowned himself in tears of despair and defeat. These would have been natural responses to the situation, but we discover John singing a doxology. From his lips is voiced a paean of praise concerning Jesus Christ. The apostle's message centers on the person of Christ (who he is), the purpose of Christ (what he has done), and the people of Christ (our response to him).

The Person of Christ

John identified Jesus Christ in a threefold manner. He is "the faithful witness, the first-born of the dead, and the ruler of kings on earth" (v. 5). Jesus Christ is "the faithful witness" because his testimony is reliable. We can believe what he says; he keeps his word. Moreover, we can trust him and not be disappointed, since he holds the key to meaningful life (John 10:10).

Jesus Christ is "the faithful witness" in a second sense. He authentically represents God the Father. Throughout the centuries people inquired, "Who is God? What is he like?" Inquisitive Philip demanded, "Lord, show us the Father, and we will be satisfied." Jesus replied, "Have I been with you so long, and yet you do not know me, Philip? He who has seen me has seen the Father" (John 14:8-9). Paul declared that Jesus Christ is "the image of the invisible God" and that "in him all the fulness of God was pleased to dwell" (Col 1:15,19). God revealed himself fully and finally in the person of Jesus of Nazareth. As we focus on the words and works of Jesus, we gain a deeper understanding of God and his purpose for our lives.

Finally, Jesus Christ is "the faithful witness" because he was faithful unto death. The Greek for "witness" is *martus,* from which we derive our term martyr. For Christians suffering in Asia Minor, Jesus Christ was the protomartyr. He refused to hoard life selfishly but willingly gave himself "as a ransom for many" (Mark 10:45). The encounter with the Greeks (John 12:20-28) and the agony of

Gethsemane (Mark 14:32-42) unmistakably reveal Jesus' inner struggle. He could have evaded the Cross, but chose not to do so. Instead, he embraced death, making it possible for us to know the forgiveness of sins and experience eternal life.

John further portrayed Jesus Christ as "the first-born of the dead." This title is found in Colossians 1:18 where Jesus is declared Lord over the church by virtue of his resurrection. The fact that he is "first-born" signifies that others will follow. He is "the first fruits of those who have fallen asleep" (1 Cor 15:20). The resurrection of Jesus is the foundation of our faith. Somewhere in Jerusalem is an empty tomb. The grave could not contain him. As the living Christ, he has "the keys of Death" (Rev 1:18). Once death resembled a desolate prison from which there was no escape. When Jesus arose, he set the prisoners free!

With the phrase, "the ruler of kings on earth," John proclaimed the Lordship of Christ. Indeed, he is "King of kings and Lord of lords" (19:16). Earthly kingdoms are under his control. World leaders have marched across the stage of history. Some have attempted to usurp the authority and power that alone belong to the Lord of Glory. Domitian assumed the place of deity, but his reign soon terminated. Napoleon proposed to conquer Russia. As the Corsican boasted, one of his officers rebuked him, "Sire, man proposes, but God disposes." Napoleon curtly replied, "I will propose, and I will dispose."[2] But the Little Corporal did not get his way. He was defeated by that frailest of all weapons, the snowflake. Hitler believed the Third Reich would last a thousand years, but it crumbled in less than twenty, closing the curtain on a dark era of human tragedy.

World systems have their day, disappear, and are soon forgotten. Behind the scenes, however, abides One exalted to the right hand of God where he reigns over all the rulers of the earth. His promised return will demonstrate the sovereignty that is rightfully his. Then every knee will bow and every tongue will confess Jesus Christ as Lord (Phil 2:10-11). At the moment, however, "we do not yet see everything in subjection to him" (Heb 2:8).

Beleaguered believers in John's day found encouragement in his vibrant message of victory. To disciples in every generation comes the challenge to share the good news that Jesus Christ is alive and reigns, and that his kingdom will stand forever. Forces of evil are on their way to defeat. Followers of Christ are on the winning team.

The Purpose of Christ

Christ's purpose is seen in three graphic verbs: "loves," "freed," and "made." The first verb is in the present tense and denotes continuing action. There is a timeless quality about Christ's love for us. Prior to creation he loved us. He was "the Lamb slain from the foundation of the world" (Rev 13:8, KJV).[3] At Calvary he loved us (John 3:16; Rom 5:8). Moreover, his love will stand the test of time. In the words of Jeremiah, "I have loved you with an everlasting love" (31:3).

Such love "has freed us from our sins." Here is love in action. It is love's nature to act. Love can no more fail to act than the sun can refuse to shine or fire can fail to burn. Frederick B. Speakman has reminded us that "love is something you do."[4] Words are cheap. The true measure of love is how one acts.

Christ acted to release us from our sins. Some translations have the word "washed." Perhaps the best manuscript evidence supports the reading "freed" or "loosed." A difference of one letter exists between the two Greek verbs. Whichever translation we follow, the meaning is basically the same. The aorist tense indicates completed action in the past time. Jesus Christ loves us continually, but he acted once for all to free us from sin and guilt. He accomplished this by his death on the Cross. The cost of our redemption was "his blood." Elsewhere we are told that Christ's blood "cleanses us from all sin" (1 John 1:7).

I read a moving story about two American fliers who were stationed in England. One day while flying at low altitude on a training mission, something went wrong with their plane. A crash was imminent. At the time, they were flying over a populated area. In fact, their plane had begun to dive toward a school. Hundreds of people, mostly children, would be hurt or killed. The pilots had to make a snap decision. One option was to parachute to safety and allow their plane to continue on its tragic course.

Their lives would be spared. The other choice was to guide the plane as best they could to a location where nobody on the ground would be affected. They chose to do the latter. By sacrificing themselves, they spared the lives of countless others. Jesus sacrificed his life for us. In love he bore our sins that we might be acquitted (2 Cor 5:21).

John climaxed his presentation of Christ's purpose with the affirmation that he has "made us a kingdom, priests to his God and Father." This statement recalls Exodus 19:6 where Israel was regarded as a "kingdom of priests and a holy nation." Early Christians believed themselves to be the true Israel, the recipients of God's inheritance (1 Pet 2:9-10).

Priesthood implies direct access to God at all times. On the day Jesus died the curtain in the temple was "torn in two, from top to bottom" (Matt 27:51), exposing the mercy seat to all people. Every believer can dare to come boldly to the throne of grace (Heb 4:16). The "dividing wall" has been "broken down" (Eph 2:14).

As priests we do not require a mediator who stands between us and God. We possess soul competency by right of creation. Therefore, we are endowed with the ability to interpret God's Word for ourselves and to determine His will for our lives. The cherished doctrine of the priesthood of the believer must never be perverted to mean that an authoritarian pastor can dictate to others what they must believe and do.

The People of Christ

Having considered the person and the purpose of Christ, John concluded with a dynamic response required by the people of Christ. It is expressed in the form of a doxology: "To him be glory and dominion for ever and ever." "Glory" translates a Greek word that serves as the root for our liturgical term "doxology." Certainly our response will include praise and worship. But glory includes much more. Lip-service will lead to life-service. Our profession of faith will result in the practice of our faith. Glory means that in our daily experience we will reflect God's image revealed in Christ.

Glory points to the visible presence of the invisible God. In the Old Testament God's glory was partial. It was manifested, for example, in the pillar of fire and the cloud in the wilderness (Exod 13:21-22). When Moses longed to see God's glory, he was told that he could not view God directly (Exod 33:17-23). The situation changed, however, with the coming of Jesus. God's visible presence was personified in his Son. The prologue of John's Gospel affirms: "And the Word became flesh and dwelt among us, full of grace and truth; we have beheld his glory, glory as of the only Son from the Father" (John 1:14). Jesus Christ became God's glory!

The final step is advanced by Paul. The apostle challenged believers "to live for the praise of his glory" (Eph 1:12). With a triumphant shout, he concluded, "Christ in you, the hope of glory" (Col 1:27). We are the continuing incarnation. Our challenge is to make visible to our world the presence of the invisible God. God will become real to others through us. They will come to know Christ by our words and our deeds.

"Dominion" means lordship. When we receive Jesus Christ as Savior, we will want to make him the Lord of our lives. He is our Master; we are his servants. He is in control. Our prayer becomes, "Thy will be done" (Matt 6:10).

A new friend and I sat together on the steps of a storefront church. The time was Sunday evening just before dark. He was probably in his early twenties. I was a college student sent out as a summer missionary. I listened as he told his story, about how he had accepted Jesus Christ as his Savior and Lord. It happened during an English language course taught by one of our missionaries. The Gospel of John was used as the text.

When the young man announced his decision to his parents, they expressed strong disapproval, "You must leave our home at once," they told him. "We don't ever want to see you again." Turned out by family and rejected by friends, he gave up his place in society and a secure financial future. He discovered for himself the meaning of Jesus' saying, "If any man would come after me, let him deny himself and take up his cross daily and follow me" (Luke 9:23).

The sound of the organ playing interrupted our conversation. It was time for the worship service to begin. As we entered the building, he added, "I made the right choice. I could never go back to the life I had before I met Christ." His eyes were bright, and a look of peace and joy radiated from his face. This young man knew the meaning of the lordship of Christ.

Do you know what you believe and why? Christian discipleship is grounded in an affirmation of faith about the person and work of Jesus Christ.

Notes

[1]Biblical quotations, unless otherwise noted, are from the Revised Standard Version of the Bible.

[2]V. J. Chitwood, *A Faith That Works* (Nashville: Broadman, 1969) 95.

[3]This rendering by the Authorized Version calls attention to the fact that God's redeeming love predated creation. Support for this is found in 1 Peter 1:18-20. Other translations connect "from the foundation of the world" with those whose names have been written "in the book of life." Support for this is derived from the parallel in Revelation 17:8 and from Ephesians 1:4. The ambiguity of the Greek text of Revelation 13:8 allows for either translation. We need not choose between the views that the the Cross was in the heart of God before creation and that God previously knew his own. Both are significant truths we embrace.

[4]This is the opening chapter in a book by the same title, *Love is Something You Do* (Westwood NJ: Fleming H. Revell, 1959). Speakman contends that love involves not so much feeling as doing.

[5]The original source of this story is unknown.

†††

Catching People

Luke 5:1-11

James A. Weaver

Someone has observed that the fastest growing thing in nature is a fish—from the time a fellow catches it until he starts to tell about it. The fisherman Simon Peter had a story that he must have told to anyone who would listen. It was a story about an astounding haul of fish he made one morning. And, no doubt, more than a few incredulous eyebrows were raised. But Simon Peter's story was no typical fish tale. It's the gospel truth. For the story isn't so much about catching fish at all but about the Kingdom getting hold of Simon Peter.

The story begins in the frustration of futility. Through an exhausting night Lake Gennesaret had yielded up nothing but empty fishing nets for Simon Peter, his brother Andrew and their partners in the seafood business, James and John, the sons of Zebedee. The weary men had just docked their boats and started the chore of cleaning their nets when some excitement broke out on the shore. Jesus, whose fame was spreading like a wild fire, was flanked by a crowd enthralled with his teaching. The beach had become an open-air classroom, and everyone wanted a front-row seat. It may have been almost a vaudeville scene—a step forward by the crowd, crushing in on Jesus; a step backward by Jesus, searching for some space to breath. And this two-step was on a collision course with the lake.

Simon Peter and his fishing partners, anxious to complete the drudgery of washing nets that had only captured slimy debris, plodded along in their task, perhaps occasionally glancing up to view the commotion. This was not the first time that Simon Peter had been around Jesus. Jesus had even been a guest in Simon Peter's house and, while he was there, he had healed Simon Peter's ill mother-in-law (Luke 4:38-39). But on this morning after, Simon

Peter's mind was on business—and probably on sleep—and he and his brother and his friends kept on tending to the nets, preparing them for another night of fishing, which they figured had to be more profitable.

About this time the shuffle to the sea had run out of sand. One more step and Jesus would begin paddling water. Jesus spied an escape route. He jumped into Simon Peter's boat, and he beckoned Simon Peter, who was now getting interested in what was going on, to come and push off a bit from the shore. And there on the lake Jesus preached and taught, the boat a floating pulpit and the water a natural amplification system.

When Jesus concluded his teaching and the crowd began to drift away, he directed his full attention to Simon Peter, who had sat there with him in the boat as a captive audience. Jesus, not so casually, suggested that Simon Peter attempt again to bring in a catch of fish. "Go out into the deep water and let your nets down," Jesus said.

We can certainly imagine what was racing through Simon Peter's mind. Here's a professional fisherman being given advice on fishing by a carpenter from Nazareth, which was no seacoast town. Maybe Jesus had built a few boats, but he plainly hadn't fished from many. It wasn't even the right time to go fishing. You fished in the cool of the night, not during the glaring daylight. Everybody knew that—everybody except, it seemed, this Jesus.

But Simon Peter was restrained in his objection, "Master, we're worn out. We have worked all night long and we didn't catch a thing." And, then, he relented, "But, sir, if you say so, I'll do it. At your instruction, I'll sail into deeper waters and let down the nets." Simon Peter followed Jesus' word with a response that falls somewhere on a sliding scale between expectant faith and skeptical obedience.

Nonetheless, Simon Peter went fishing again. He had, after all, seen Jesus' miracle-working power when he healed his mother-in-law. Who's to say what might have happened if he was obedient to this Jesus. And, anyway, it surely wouldn't hurt to try one more time to catch some fish. After all, the boat was already back out on the lake. So Simon Peter navigated into the deep water and threw the nets over the side of the boat.

Before he had time to grow impatient, his nets had enclosed a tremendous school of fish. Frantically, Simon Peter and Andrew, who was also in the boat, wrestled with the nets, desperately attempting to keep them from breaking open. They motioned excitedly with their arms and shouted for James and John to hurry with their boat to assist them. The catch was so successful that both boats groaned under the weight of the fish and dipped level with the waves of the sea.

But even in the midst of all of this confusion, Simon Peter perceived that something more than an amazing display of fisherman's luck was occurring. He had the presence of mind to realize that he stood in a matchless presence, the presence of this Jesus, who had spoken the word to put out into the deep water. And Simon Peter dropped in the boat at Jesus' knees, in the middle of the belly-flopping fish, and he cried out, "Go away from me, Lord, for I am a sinful man."

That may seem like a peculiar thing for Simon Peter to utter in the frenzy of a fishing expedition unlike any he had ever witnessed. But he wasn't offering some embarrassed apology for doubting whether Jesus had known what he was talking about when he gave his counsel on catching fish. Simon Peter's plaintive plea was the confession of a person who knew that he had encountered someone unique, someone extraordinary, and Simon Peter was overwhelmed by his own unworthiness and inadequacy to be near him. Simon Peter sensed that he had come fact to face with One who belonged to the transcendent realm of the divine— the holy. And in the dazzling, piercing light of holiness, which exposes everything, Simon Peter could not conceal nor stand what he saw of himself. And so he fell down with his penitent cry.

We hear this word holy, and we think most often of a way of morality, of a style of life. But holy living only issues from a particular kind of being. Holiness, at its root, means to be separate. Holiness signifies "the uniqueness, the distinctness, the one-of-a-kindness," the cannot-be-duplicated quality of a person or object.[1] To say that God is holy is to say that God is nothing like humanity. God is absolutely different from anything or anyone else. Nothing can be placed alongside God in comparison. God is the One who is Wholly Other. From this fundamental truth about God all other truth about God derives.

To confront the presence of the Holy God is to be made starkly aware of our frailties, our inadequacies, our limitations, our sins. It is to be jolted into the recognition that we are only finite creatures—we always have been, we always will be. It is to be shamed by our half-hearted commitments and shallow loyalties. It is to be embarrassed by our petty concerns and trivial pursuits. It is to be confronted by our unworthiness to be in the presence of such a Holy One.

This was the experience of Moses at the burning bush. This was the experience of Isaiah in the temple as he lamented, "Woe is me, for I am lost; I am a man of unclean lips." This was the experience of Simon Peter, who begged, "Go away from me, Lord, for I am a sinful man." This must be the experience of anyone who authentically encounters the presence of the Holy God.

The tragedy is that the perception of God's holiness has virtually vanished in contemporary life. There is not much wonder at the incomparable otherness of God. Awe is not a quality much cultivated anymore. If the secular world pauses in reverence at anything, it is technology. Folks believe that the ingenuity of the human mind can solve any problem, given enough time and money.

And the religious world doesn't have much wonder at the holiness of God either. We have pared God down to size—our size. God becomes our pal, our buddy, something like the jolly neighbor next door who we are sure is always there when we need him, but somehow we have never really gotten to know him. There is a superficial, an artificial, intimacy.

With this kind of cozy God worship lapses into entertainment. The call to repentance becomes an advertisement for a seminar in self-help. Churches cater to consumers rather than make servant disciples. The pilgrimage of faith becomes a sentimental journey.

Centuries ago King Ethelbert of Kent gave an audience to some Christian missionaries, yet only out of doors, because he lived in fearful awe of the wondrous, mysterious deed that might be worked through these bearers of the gospel inside the castle.[2] But

Annie Dillard describes more our modern mood of insensibility to the holy power of God:

> On the whole, I do not find Christians, outside of the catacombs, sufficiently sensible of conditions. Does anyone have the foggiest idea what sort of power we so blithely invoke? Or, as I suspect, does no one believe a word of it? The churches are children playing on the floor with their chemistry sets, mixing up a batch of TNT to kill a Sunday morning. It is madness to wear ladies' straw hats and velvet hats to church; we should all be wearing crash helmets. Ushers should issue life preservers and signal flares; they should lash us to our pews.[3]

But we amble in and out of the presence of the God we perceive, untouched and unscathed.

This kind of God has a certain attraction for many of us. We can keep this kind of God under control. This kind of God is familiar, and there is a complacent security and easy comfort in familiarity. We are always sure of what to expect. There are no surprises. There is no mystery. In fact, we find that this kind of God begins to look just like us and to mirror our values and priorities. We are convinced that this kind of God has let us in on all of the divine secrets. And we may dare to become so bold as to claim that we, and we alone, speak for God.

This kind of God makes few demands on us. Maybe that's why this kind of God has such an appeal. We don't have to take off our shoes on holy ground, like Moses. We don't have to mumble through blistered lips, like Isaiah. We don't have to do a dive to our knees in a tossing boat of smelly fish, like Simon Peter. With this kind of God we pull up a lounge chair and remind God of how fortunate God is to have us. We decide whether it's convenient for us to do what this kind of God asks us to do. And if we choose to do something else or nothing at all, it's no big deal. After all, we're such good buddies with this kind of God that even if we do slip up a bit, God will just grin and wink and look the other way.

But this kind of God is not the Holy God of the Scriptures. This kind of God is not the God who confronted Simon Peter in Jesus the Christ. And Simon Peter realized that. Simon Peter knew better. And he fell down, and cried, "Go away from me, Lord, for I am a sinful man"—too sinful to be in your holy presence.

But Jesus didn't go away. He stayed right there because God is a God whose holiness is expressed in grace. Jesus offered Simon Peter genuine intimacy with him, which effects real transformation of life. Not a word was said to Simon Peter about forgiveness. But forgiveness was active. It came in a word of assurance. "Don't be afraid," Jesus declared. There was no reason to fear anymore.

And then came the commissioning. "From now on you will be catching people," Jesus said to Simon Peter. Whenever someone has encountered the holiness of God and experienced the forgiveness of God and been drawn into authentic intimacy with God, there has to be a commission from God. It happened to Moses, and he went back to Egypt and rescued his people. It happened to Isaiah, and he volunteered, "Here am I; send me." It happened to Simon Peter. "From now on," Jesus said, in a word that was both prospect and responsibility, "you will be catching people."

"From now on." A turning point had occurred. Something—Someone—had happened to Simon Peter. While Simon Peter had been dragging fish over fish into his sinking boat, Jesus had been doing some fishing of his own. And Simon Peter had been caught for the Kingdom. He had become a disciple of Jesus. And "from now on" he would invest his life in what Jesus was doing in the world. It could be no other way, for true disciples are those who do what Jesus does.

And that meant Simon Peter himself was to be about catching people for the Kingdom of God. Jesus told Simon Peter, quite literally, that he would be "taking people alive." People would be snatched from death and preserved for life, netted together as God's people, followers in the Kingdom.[4]

This promise of catching people is the real miracle in the story. As a fisher of people for the Kingdom, if Simon Peter relied on his own human resources, he would be no more successful than he had been in that futile night on the lake, trying to gather fish into his boat. But Simon Peter had been bowled over by his sense of unworthiness and by the recognition of his absolute dependence upon the One who is holy. And Simon Peter opened his life to become a conduit of the miracles of transformation that flow from the reservoir of the Kingdom. Through the power of Jesus the Christ, Simon Peter had caught fish like never before. Now through the power of Jesus the Christ, Simon Peter would just as assuredly catch people and direct them to the holy, gracious, forgiving God that they, too, might experience the dynamic work of redemption.

Here the story reaches its straightforward conclusion. The mission had been presented in crystal clarity. The boats docked again on the beach, and not just Simon Peter, but also Andrew and James and John left everything, including two boats overloaded with enough fish to keep their business in the black for a long time—and they followed Jesus. They still had so much to learn about Jesus. They had no idea what even the next day held for them. But they knew that more than anything else they wanted to be—they had to be—with Jesus. They said Yes to following Jesus, whatever that would mean, wherever that would take them, whatever it would cost them—even their lives. That unconditional response of affirmation is the essence of discipleship.

And the call to be a disciple—a follower—of Jesus has always been, as it was for Simon Peter, a commissioning to serve. There is the commission to be a fisher of people, or a carpenter of people, or an educator of people, or an accountant of people, or a medical technician of people, or a sales representative to people, or whatever it is that we do in the ordinary, daily course of life where Jesus comes to us and bids us to follow him and gather people into the Kingdom. To accept the call to follow Jesus is also to embrace the commission to be a servant in the work of Jesus.[5]

This dual call and commission of Jesus—that is really one—has not changed since it was issued to Simon Peter. And to respond means to be seized in wonder by the mysterious holiness of the One who calls us and to serve in obedience through the incomparable power of the One who commissions us.

Of that much, I am sure. But there is something I cannot say—everything that all of this will mean to each one of us as we follow Jesus the Christ faithfully in our own particular lives. And there is something I cannot do—compel any of us to heed the call and to accept the commission.

But this I also know. This call to follow—this commission to serve—comes to all of us, without exception. And your life, my life, every life is at stake.

Notes

[1]John Claypool, *Glad Reunion: Meeting Ourselves in the Lives of the Bible Men and Women* (Waco: Word Books, 1985) 135.

[2]Roland H. Bainton, *The Church of Our Father* (New York: Charles Scribner's Sons, 1969) 78.

[3]Annie Dillard, *Teaching a Stone to Talk: Expeditions and Encounters* (New York: Harper & Row, 1982) 40.

[4]Joseph A. Fitzmyer, *The Gospel According to Luke I-IX*, Anchor Bible 28 (Garden City NY: Doubleday and Company, 1981) 563.

[5]Charles H. Talert, *Reading Luke: A Literary and Theological Commentary on the Third Gospel* (New York: Crossroad, 1982) 61, says, "The merging of call and commissioning in 5:1-11 reflects the view that to be called to be a disciple is at the same time to be commissioned as a fisher."

†††

Possessions

Luke 14:33, 19:8-9

Kenneth Wolfe

Whoever of you does not renounce all that he has cannot be my disciple. (Luke 14:33)

And Zacchaeus stood and said to the Lord, "Behold, Lord, the half of my goods I give to the poor; and if I have defrauded any one of anything I restore it fourfold." And Jesus said to him, "Today salvation has come to this house. . . ." (Luke 19:8-9)

These two texts represent two facets of Jesus' teachings in the Gospel of Luke. In the first text Jesus says that one must renounce everything that he or she has to become his disciple. The second tells the story of a man who, upon encountering Jesus, announces his intention to give half of his goods to the poor and to repay fourfold anyone he has defrauded. In response to this decision Jesus declares, "Today salvation has come to this house. . . ." The first text demands that one must renounce all of one's possessions to become a disciple of Jesus, the second endorses a generous and prudent usage of one's possessions to help the poor, along with restitution to those whom one has exploited. These two antithetical texts represent recurring themes in the Gospel of Luke and the book of Acts. They pose the difficult and perplexing question about the relationship between a disciple of Jesus and possessions.

These statements are set in the larger context of the thoroughgoing identification of Jesus with the poor. This theme is already in evidence in the birth narratives in Luke. The birth of Jesus, in Luke, takes place among lowly people. Unlike Matthew, who does not mention the place of Jesus' birth, Luke tells about the child being born in a stable. In contrast with the astrologers from the east who bring their luxurious gifts in Matthew's narrative, lowly shepherds visit the new born child in Luke's narrative. Matthew's narrative focuses upon the men involved, Joseph and Herod, whereas Luke's narrative tells the story of the women involved, Mary and Elizabeth. Mary's hymn celebrating the gift of the child begins with a reference to her lowly estate and goes on to describe how God has put down the mighty and exalted those of low degree. She sings of those who are hungry being filled and the rich being sent away empty.

In the preaching of Jesus in Luke Jesus highlights his mission to the poor. In this Gospel the sermon of Jesus in his own home town, Nazareth, is placed in a prominent position at the very beginning of his ministry. Luke has made this passage the epitome of his Gospel. In the sermon Jesus reads from the prophet Isaiah:

> The Spirit of the Lord is upon me, because he has anointed me to preach good news to the poor. He has sent me to proclaim release to the captives and recovering of sight to the blind, to set at liberty those who are oppressed, to proclaim the acceptable year of the Lord. (Luke 4:18-19)

In dramatic fashion Jesus rolls up the scroll, sits down and announces, "Today this scripture has been fulfilled in your hearing." Jesus sees his mission as that of bringing both good news and deliverance to those who are poor, to those who are captives, to those who are blind, and to those who are oppressed. The acceptable year of the Lord was the year of Jubilee commanded in Leviticus 25. On this fiftieth year debts were to be forgiven and those who had become poor and had sold themselves as slaves were to be freed. Land that had been sold was to be returned to its original owner. Jesus has been anointed by the Spirit of God to embody the divine compassion for the poor and the oppressed. This passage is the key to understanding the ministry that follows.

Both Matthew and Luke place the great sermon of Jesus on discipleship just after the call of the disciples. Luke positions Jesus with his disciples in the midst of the crowd. At the beginning of the sermon he tells us that Jesus looks up at his disciples. He begins the sermon by addressing the poor. The poor obviously include the disciples who have abandoned all to follow him. But the poor he ministers to are those who are poor because of the circumstances of life. He speaks directly to the poor, "Blessed are you poor, for yours is the kingdom of God." "You hungry will be full and you who weep now will laugh," he tells them. The rich are told that they have received their consolation. The full shall be hungry and those who laugh shall cry. This sermon reflects the same reversal of the positions of the poor and the rich as that reflected in Mary's song. It is the prime example in Luke of Jesus preaching "good news to the poor."

Jesus points to his ministry to the blind, the lame, lepers, the deaf, the dead and his announcement of good news to the poor as evidence that he is the long awaited redeemer. When John sends two of his disciples to ask Jesus whether he is really the one they have been expecting, Jesus sends them back to John to tell him what they have seen and heard: "the blind receive their sight, the lame walk, lepers are cleansed, and the deaf hear, the dead are raised up, the poor have good news preached to them." These concrete deeds of compassion toward the sick, the blind, the suffering, and the poor are evidence that he is the bearer of the long awaited deliverance. These deeds represent the carrying out of the commission announced at Nazareth.

Luke, like Matthew, has Jesus tell a parable about a great banquet that the invited guests refuse to attend. In the parable in Luke's narrative when the invited guests make their excuses, the host of the banquet sends his servant out to bring in the "poor and maimed and blind and lame" (Luke 14:21). Probably the parable in Luke is an allegory of the mission of Jesus. After those who are first invited do not accept the invitation, Jesus turns to the poor and afflicted. After these are brought in the servants are sent into the highways and hedges to compel others to come to the banquet, perhaps the Gentiles. This parable, like the teachings of Jesus already considered, demonstrates the thoroughgoing identification of Jesus with the poor and needy. He sees himself as being sent to the poor, the sick, the oppressed. It is in this context that Luke places the call to discipleship.

There are several incidents in Luke's narrative where Jesus' call to discipleship entails a renunciation of all of one's possessions.

What is striking in these accounts is the way Luke emphasizes that *everything* must be forsaken.

In the call of the fishermen, Simon and the sons of Zebedee, Mark and Matthew mention that these men left their nets, their boat and their father and followed Jesus. Luke writes that they left *everything* and followed him (5:11).

Luke has the same word and the same emphasis in his narrative of the call of Levi. Mark and Matthew merely say that Levi rose and followed Jesus (Mark 2:14, Matt 9:9). Luke writes that he left *everything* and followed Jesus (5:28).

At the end of a series of sayings of Jesus about the great demands set upon those who would become his disciples, Luke has the saying about forsaking *everything* that one possesses to become his disciple (Luke 14:33). These sayings are addressed to the multitudes. Jesus indicates that one cannot be his disciple unless one is willing to turn's one's back on (hate) family and even life itself and bear his or her own cross. At the climax of these sayings Jesus says "Whoever of you does not part with *everything* that he or she possesses cannot be my disciple." Though the translations do not always clearly stress it, the word "everything" or "all" is found in this saying also. It is connected to the word possessions in the original language. It is a demand to say good-bye to everything one possesses. And it is not directed just to the twelve, it is addressed to the multitudes. It is a demand made on "everyone" who would become a disciple.

In Luke's telling of the unsuccessful call of the rich ruler he again emphasizes the demand to sell *everything* one has in order to become a disciple. Once again he has the word "everything" where the other two evangelists do not have it. Both Mark and Matthew have the call to the wealthy man to sell what he has or possesses and give to the poor (Mark 10:21, Matt 19:21). In Luke's version of this saying, he has Jesus say, "Sell *everything* that you have and distribute to the poor" (Luke 18:22). The question of this rich person is about what he must do to inherit eternal life. Jesus' demand is in response to that question.

Alongside these demands to abandon all of one's possessions there are other incidents or sayings in Luke's narrative that present a different understanding of Jesus' teachings about possessions. In this second type of saying Jesus does not demand the giving up of all of one's possessions, but rather an appropriate usage of possessions.

In chapter fourteen there is an account of Jesus dining at the home of a Pharisee who was a ruler. Those who had been invited were choosing the places of honor. After admonishing a humbler attitude Jesus turns to the host and tells him not to invite his friends or kinsmen or rich neighbors who could repay the favor. Rather, he admonishes, invite "the poor, the maimed, the lame, the blind." The parable about the great banquet in which the well-to-do were invited but did not come follows this incident. The same words, "the poor and maimed and blind and lame," are used to describe those invited to the banquet in the parable.

Zacchaeus is the prime example of one who experiences the salvation of Jesus without renouncing all of his possessions. The location of this story in the narrative is significant. It is placed at the end of the lengthy journey to Jerusalem and at the end of Jesus' public ministry. Almost immediately after this story Jesus arrives at Bethany and the Mount of Olives and moves into Jerusalem for the culmination of his mission. This is Jesus' last public act. It touches on significant themes in Luke's Gospel, the relationship between Jesus and the tax collectors and Jesus and the rich. It seems to be the climax of the development of the theme of Jesus' mission to the poor and the outcasts. It is extremely significant for understanding Luke's development of these themes.

The response of Zacchaeus to his encounter with Jesus is unexpected and significant. It reflects Luke's view of the nature of salvation and of discipleship. Discipleship has a social and an economic dimension. Zacchaeus does not make a statement about who he believes Jesus to be. He does not even ask for forgiveness for having exploited the helpless. He rather stands up and says that he is going to give half of his goods to the poor and that he is going to restore fourfold any he has defrauded. And in response to this dramatic decision Jesus declares that salvation has come to the house of Zacchaeus. And Luke adds, "For the Son of man came to seek and to save the lost" (Luke 19:10).

There is continuity between the concern for the poor and the sharing of one's possessions with the poor portrayed in the Gospel of Luke and that portrayed in the Book of Acts. The first glimpse Luke gives of the life of the young church is that of a community that "had all things in common." It is a picture of a church in which those with possessions were selling their possessions to provide for those who were needy as needs arose (Acts 2:45). Luke gives a noble example of those who sell their property, Barnabas, and a not so noble example, Ananias and Sapphira.

The church was systematically providing for the needs of the widows in its midst (Acts 6:1-6). The disciples in Antioch in Syria send relief to the disciples in Judea during a time of famine (Acts 11:27-30). Another extensive relief effort for the people of Palestine is mentioned in Acts 24:17. Tabitha is noted for her good works and acts of charity (Acts. 9:36). Cornelius and his household give alms liberally to those in need (Acts 10:2).

As Paul begins his last journey to Jerusalem, knowing that he faces imprisonment and suffering, he makes a farewell speech to the Elders at Ephesus. He reminds them of his example of toiling to help the weak. He ends his speech with a striking quote from Jesus about possessions, "It is more blessed to give than to receive" (Acts 20:35).

On some occasions Jesus demands that one renounce all of his possessions in order to become his disciple. On other occasions he exhorts those with possessions to share them with the poor or he affirms one who shares half of his possessions with the poor and who makes generous restitution to any he has defrauded. The disciples in the early church as depicted in Acts share their possessions, sometimes selling their property, with those in need.

What does this paradox mean for our discipleship? Apparently in the church of Luke's time there was no demand that the disciple sell all of his or her possessions. However, the solidarity with the poor is still in evidence. In the book of Acts those who have means share with those who are needy.

The God Jesus reveals is a God who identifies with the poor. He is a God who hears the cries of the oppressed. Jesus' alleviation of the sufferings of the poor, their blindness, lameness and sickness, and his promise that the hungry will be full demonstrates His rejection of these conditions of poverty and affliction. If we are to be disciples of Jesus we must align ourselves with the struggles of the oppressed and the poor. Without doubt this means providing for their needs to the extent we are able. It probably also means opposing those forces that create the oppression.

The young church was seeking to spread its message to the ends of the earth. It was comprised of small communities who were very much in the minority. These communities had not turned to the problems of injustice that created the poverty and suffering. They did not even oppose slavery. It is up to us to determine what the implications of the solidarity of Jesus with the poor and oppressed mean for our discipleship. Are not the movements to liberate the oppressed, including women, in our society an expression of the divine concern for those who are downtrodden? Is not the far reaching movement among the churches in South America to obtain liberty for the poor an evidence of the moving of the spirit of God in our midst? Could it be that our distance from and even unawareness of these movements and concerns is a symptom of how far we have distanced ourselves from the Gospel? Could it be that we have separated ourselves from what the divine Spirit is doing in our day?

†††

Contributors

Fred W. Andrea is the Senior Pastor of the First Baptist Church of Aiken, South Carolina. He has been pastor of the First Baptist Church of Savannah, Georgia (1989–1993) and the Augusta Heights Baptist Church of Greenville, South Carolina (1983–1989). He holds degrees from Clemson University (B.A.) and The Southern Baptist Theological Seminary (M.Div., Ph.D.). He compiled *Shooting the Rapids: Effective Ministry in a Changing World* and has contributed to *The Minister's Manual*, the *Manual for Preaching and Worship Planning*, and many denominational publications and sermon collections.

Gerald Borchert is the T. Rupert and Lucille Coleman Professor of New Testament Interpretation at The Southern Baptist Theological Seminary in Louisville, Kentucky where he has taught since 1980. Prior to this he was Professor of New Testament and Dean at Northern Baptist Seminary in Lombard, Illinois and at North American Baptist Seminary in Sioux Falls, South Dakota. He holds degrees from the University of Alberta (B.A., LL.B.), Eastern Baptist Theological Seminary (M.Div.), and Princeton Theological Seminary (Th.M., Ph.D.). A frequent contributor to a wide variety of journals and periodicals, his published books include *Great Themes from John, Dynamics of Evangelism, Paul and His Interpreters, Discovering Thessalonians, Assurance and Warning: The Balance in 1 Corinthians, John and Hebrews.* He is presently completing commentaries on the Gospel of John for the *New American Commentary* and the *Mercer Commentary on the Bible.*

Linda McKinnish Bridges is Associate Professor of New Testament and Greek at the Baptist Theological Seminary of Richmond, Virginia. She has served as a visiting professor at Union Theological Seminary in Richmond, the Lexington Theological Seminary in Kentucky, and The Southern Baptist Theological Seminary. She served as a missionary to Taiwan from 1977–1982. Dr. Bridges holds degrees from Meredith College (B.A.) and The Southern Baptist Theological Seminary (M.Div., Ph.D.). She has contributed articles to a wide variety of scholarly journals and has written the commentary on 1 and 2 Thessalonians for the *Mercer Commentary* *of the Bible.* She is presently completing work on *The Church's Portrait of Jesus in the Four Gospels,* a book in a series of eight volumes in the Guide to the Bible Series for Smyth and Helwys.

Donald E. Cook is Senior Professor of New Testament Interpretation at The Divinity School of Gardner-Webb University in Boiling Springs, North Carolina. He has also served as a professor of New Testament at Southeastern Theological Seminary since 1965. He holds degrees from Furman University (B.A.), Southeastern Baptist Theological Seminary (B.D., Th.M.), and Duke University (Ph.D.). He has also studied at the Hebrew Union Seminary in Jerusalem, Israel. Dr. Cook has written a variety of curriculum materials for the Sunday School Board of the Southern Baptist Convention and authored numerous articles for scholarly journals.

Bruce Corley is the Dean of the School of Theology of the Southwestern Baptist Theological Seminary where he has been Professor of New Testament since 1976. He holds degrees from Northeastern Oklahoma State University (B.S. Ed.) and Southwestern Seminary (M.Div., Th.D.). He has done post-graduate study at Cambridge University and Kings College of the University of Aberdeen. A frequent contributor to the *Southwestern Journal of Theology* and the *Biblical Illustrator,* he has edited *Colloquy on New Testament Studies* and co-authored commentaries on Romans and 2 Corinthians. He is presently completing a commentary on Hebrews for the *New American Commentary.*

R. Alan Culpepper is Professor of New Testament at Baylor University. Prior to joining the faculty there in 1992, he had served as Professor of New Testament at The Southern Baptist Theological Seminary since 1974. He holds degrees from Baylor University (B.A.), The Southern Baptist Theological Seminary (M.Div.), and Duke University (Ph.D.), and has done post-graduate study at Cambridge University. A prolific writer, he is a frequent contributor to a host of scholarly journals and periodicals and a regular writer of curriculum materials for use in the churches. His published books include *The Johannine School; Anatomy of the Fourth*

Gospel; John, the Son of Zebedee: The Life of a Legend; and *1, 2, 3 John*.
He is currently completing work on "The Gospel of Luke" in *The
New Interpreter's Bible*. He serves as New Testament editor for the
"Smyth and Helwys Bible Commentaries" and is writing the com-
mentary on the Gospel of Mark for that series.

Paul D. Duke has been Pastor of the Kirkwood Baptist church in
St. Louis, Missouri since 1986. Prior to this he was pastor of the
Highland Baptist Church in Louisville, Kentucky (1982–1986) and
the Burks Branch Baptist Church in Shelbyville, Kentucky
(1977–1980). He has also served as an adjunct professor of preaching at The Southern Baptist Theological Seminary and Midwestern
Baptist Theological Seminary. He holds degrees from Samford
University (B.A.) and The Southern Baptist Theological Seminary
(M.Div., Ph.D.). The author of *Irony in the Fourth Gospel* and co-
author of *Anguish and the Word: Preaching That Touches Pain*, he has
contributed sermons to numerous anthologies and articles to a
variety of periodicals and journals. Dr. Duke has been honored as
the H. I. Lecturer on Preaching at Golden Gate Theological Seminary (1988) and Midwestern Baptist Theological Seminary (1989).

David E. Garland is the Ernest and Mildred Hogan Professor of
New Testament at The Southern Baptist Theological Seminary in
Louisville, Kentucky where he has taught since 1975. He holds
degrees from The Southern Baptist Theological Seminary (M.Div.,
Ph.D.) and Oklahoma Baptist University (B.A.), and he has done
post-graduate study at Eberhard-Karls University in Tübingen,
Germany and Macquarrie University in Australia. In addition to
numerous journal and dictionary articles, Dr. Garland is the author
of *The Intention of Matthew 23*, *A Hundred Years of Study of the
Passion Narrative*, and *Reading Matthew: A Literary and Theological
Commentary on the First Gospel* and co-author of *Seeking the
Kingdom, Beyond Companionship: Christians in Marriage*, and *For
Better or Worse*.

W. Hulitt Gloer is Professor of New Testament at Midwestern
Baptist Theological Seminary in Kansas City, Missouri where he
has taught since 1983. Prior to this he was Assistant Professor of

New Testament at North American Baptist Seminary in Sioux Falls, South Dakota. He holds degrees from Baylor University (B.A.), Pittsburgh Theological Seminary (M.Div.), and The Southern Baptist Theological Seminary (Ph.D.). He is editor of *Jesus Christ, the Man from Nazareth and the Exalted Lord* and *Eschatology and the New Testament* and has contributed to a variety of journals and periodicals. He has written the commentary on 2 Corinthians in the *Mercer Commentary on the Bible* and is writing the volume on Matthew for "Smyth and Helwys Bible Commentaries."

John H. Hewett was most recently Pastor of the First Baptist Church of Asheville, North Carolina. Prior to this he was Pastor of the Kirkwood Baptist Church in St. Louis, Missouri and the Graefenburg Baptist Church and the Elmburg Baptist Church in Kentucky. He holds degrees from Stetson University (B.A.) and The Southern Baptist Theological Seminary (M.Div., Ph.D.). The author of *After Suicide*, Dr. Hewitt has also contributed to a variety of professional journals. He served as the first Moderator of the Cooperative Baptist Fellowship.

D. Leslie Hollon has been pastor of Wornall Road Baptist Church, Kansas City, since 1985. From 1978 to 1985 he was pastor of Finchville Baptist Church in Finchville, Kentucky. A graduate of Baylor University in Waco, Texas, he holds the M.Div., Th.M., and Ph.D. degrees from Southern Seminary, Louisville, Kentucky, and has done special studies at several other institutions. He has served as an adjunct professor at Midwestern Seminary; William Jewell College, Liberty, Missouri; Central Baptist Theological Seminary in Kansas City, Kansas; and The Baptist Theological Seminary in Limuru, Kenya. Dr. Hollon writes in the areas of spiritual development and worship, and recently contributed to the Smyth and Helwys book, *A Cloud of Witnesses: Sermon Illustrations and Devotionals from the Christian Heritage*.

David M. Hughes has served as Pastor of the First Baptist Church of Winston-Salem, North Carolina since May, 1991. Previous pastorates include the First Baptist Church at Elkin, North Carolina

(1984–1991) and the Bagdad Baptist Church, Bagdad, Kentucky (1982–1984). He holds degrees from Wake Forest University (B.A.), Princeton Theological Seminary (M.Div.), and The Southern Baptist Theological Seminary (Ph.D.). Dr. Hughes is active in the work of the Baptist Center for Ethics and has contributed to a variety of journals and periodicals.

Peter Rhea Jones has been pastor of the First Baptist Church of Decatur, Georgia since 1979. Prior to assuming this pastorate he served as a professor of New Testament at The Southern Baptist Theological Seminary from 1968–1979. He holds degrees from Union University in Jackson, Tennessee (B.A.), University of Mississippi (M.A.), Princeton Theological Seminary (Th.M.), and The Southern Baptist Theological Seminary (M.Div., Ph.D.). A frequent contributor to denominational publications, Dr. Jones has also published articles in a variety of professional scholarly journals. He is the author of *The Teacher of the Parables*, which he is currently revising.

Michael Martin is Associate Professor of New Testament Interpretation at Golden Gate Baptist Seminary in Mill Valley, California where he has taught since 1984. He was Assistant Professor at California Baptist College from 1981–1984. He holds degrees from Dallas Baptist College (B.A.) and Southwestern Baptist Theological Seminary (M.Div., Ph.D.). Dr. Martin is a regular contributor to the *Biblical Illustrator* and has contributed several articles in the *Holman Bible Dictionary*. In addition to writing curriculum materials for the Baptist Sunday School Board, he is completing work on a commentary on 1 and 2 Thessalonians for *New American Commentary*.

David M. May is Visiting Professor of New Testament at Midwestern Baptist Theological Seminary in Kansas City, Missouri. He held the Baptist Chair of Bible at Central Missouri State University from 1987–1990. He holds degrees from Northwest Missouri State University (B.A.) and The Southern Baptist Theological Seminary (M.Div., Ph.D.). Dr. May is active in the Society of Biblical Literature and is a member of The Contest Group:

Project on the Bible in Its Cultural Environment. His work, *The Social Scientific Study of the New Testament: A Bibliography*, is a standard reference work in this field. He contributed numerous articles to the *Mercer Dictionary of the Bible* and is a frequent contributor to a variety of journals and periodicals.

H. Stephen Shoemaker has been Pastor of the Broadway Baptist Church in Ft. Worth, Texas since 1992. Prior to this he was Pastor of the Crescent Hill Baptist Church in Louisville, Kentucky (1981–1992) and the Beverly Hills Baptist Church in Asheville, North Carolina (1978–1981). He holds degrees from Stetson University (B.A.), Union Theological Seminary (M.Div.), and The Southern Baptist Theological Seminary (Ph.D.). Dr. Shoemaker's published works include *Re-telling the Biblical Story: The Theology and Practice of Narrative Preaching*, *The Jekyll and Hyde Syndrome: A New Encounter with the Seven Deadly Sins and Seven Lively Virtues*, and *Strength in Weakness: A Lyrical Re-presentation of II Corinthians*, as well as numerous periodical articles.

R. Wayne Stacy has been the Senior Minister of the First Baptist church of Raleigh, North Carolina since 1991. Prior to this he was Associate Professor of New Testament Studies at Midwestern Baptist Theological Seminary in Kansas City, Missouri (1986–1991) and Professor of Biblical Studies and Philosophy of Palm Beach Atlantic College in West Palm Beach, Florida (1985–1986). He has also served as Pastor of the North Stuart Baptist Church in Stuart, Florida (1980–1986) and the First Baptist Church of Austin, Indiana (1974–1980). He delivered the Huriburi Preaching Lectures at McMaster University Divinity College, Hamilton, Ontario, Canada in 1983 and The Preston Lectures in Biblical Studies at Meredith College in Raleigh, North Carolina in 1992. He is a frequent contributor to a variety of journals and periodicals.

Jon M. Stubblefield has been Pastor of the First Baptist Church at Shreveport, Louisiana since 1988. Prior to this he was pastor of the Walnut Street Baptist Church in Louisville, Kentucky (1986–1988) and the Central Baptist Church in Magnolia, Arkansas (1977–1986). He holds degrees from the University of Arkansas (B.A., M.A.) and

The Southern Baptist Theological Seminary (M.Div., Ph.D.). He is a frequent writer of curriculum material for the Baptist Sunday School Board and a frequent contributor to a variety of denominational publications. His sermon "The Promise of Paradise Regained" (Isa 11:1-9) appeared in *Interpreting Isaiah for Preaching and Teaching*.

James A. Weaver has been the Pastor of the First Baptist Church of Madisonville, Kentucky since 1990. Prior to this he served as Pastor of the Arden First Baptist Church in Arden, North Carolina (1984–1990) and the Bear Creek Baptist Church in Scipio, Indiana (1979–1984). Dr. Weaver holds degrees from Wake forest University (B.A.) and The Southern Baptist Theological Seminary (M.Div., Ph.D.). In addition to the present volume, he was a contributor to *A Cloud of Witnesses: Sermon Illustrations and Devotionals from the Christian Heritage*.

Kenneth R. Wolfe has been Professor of New Testament Interpretation and Greek at Midwestern Baptist Theological Seminary in Kansas City, Missouri since 1966. He holds the B.D., Th.M., and Th.D. degrees from Central Baptist Seminary in Kansas City, Kansas. Prior to joining the faculty at Midwestern, Professor Wolfe was a missionary in Brazil. He taught in the Baptist seminary in Rio de Janeiro and helped found a Protestant (Baptist) church in Leblon, the most affluent section of Rio. While a student at Central Baptist Theological Seminary in Kansas City, he was pastor of a mission in an underprivileged section of Kansas City, the so-called East Bottoms. Reading the biography of the great Japanese Christian, Kagawa, inspired him to witness to the rich in Leblon in an attempt to minister to the poor and oppressed.